# The Independent Group

# THE INDEPENDENT GROUP

Modernism and mass culture in Britain, 1945–59

Anne Massey

**Manchester University Press**   Manchester and New York

distributed exclusively in the USA and Canada by St Martin's Press

*Published by* Manchester University Press
Oxford Road, Manchester M13 9NR, UK
*and* Room 400, 175 Fifth Avenue, New York, NY 10010, USA

*Distributed exclusively in the USA and Canada*
*by* St Martin's Press, Inc., 175 Fifth Avenue, New York, NY 10010, USA

*British Library Cataloguing-in-Publication Data*
A catalogue record is available from the British Library

*Library of Congress Cataloguing-in-Publication Data*
Massey, Anne.
     The Independent Group : modernism and mass culture in Britain,
     1945–1959 / Anne Massey.
          p.   cm.
     Includes bibliographical references (p.   ).
     ISBN 0-7190-4244-5 (hardback). – ISBN 0-7190-4245-3 (pbk.)
          1.  Independent Group (Association: Great Britain) – History.
     2.  Modernism (Art) – Great Britain.   3.  Popular culture – Great Britain.
     4.  Art, British.   5.  Art, Modern – 20th century – Great Britain.   I.  Title.
     N6768.5.I53M37   1995                                        95-3509
     709'.41 – dc20                                                   CIP

ISBN 0 7190 4244 5 *hardback*
        0 7190 4245 3 *paperback*

First published 1995
99 98 97 96 95      10 9 8 7 6 5 4 3 2 1

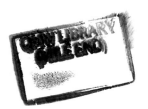

Typeset by Servis Filmsetting Ltd, Manchester
Printed in Great Britain
by Redwood Books, Trowbridge

# Contents

# List of figures

## Credits

Tyne and Wear Museums Service 4: Penrose Film Production 8: Janet Henderson
11: ICA Archives 5, 7, 9, 11, 14, 15, 16, 17, 20, 21, 22, 25, 29: Tate Gallery London 6,
12, 13: © Richard Hamilton 1995, all rights reserved, DACS 18, 26, 43, 45, 46, 47,
48: Eduardo Paolozzi 19, 44: Magda Cordell McHale 27, 36: Hatton Gallery,
Newcastle University 30, 31, 32: Research Centre for Consumer Culture 33, 34:
Whitechapel Art Gallery, London 38, 39, 40: Peter Smithson 42: Motoring Picture
Library, Beaulieu 49, 50.

# Acknowledgements

Thanks are due to Kenneth McConkey and Dr Penny Sparke who were the supervisors of the original doctoral thesis, *The Independent Group: Towards a Redefinition* (1985). Without their endless encouragement, advice and support this project would never have been realised. Thanks are also due to Dr Andrew Causey for his advice as examiner of the thesis. All three encouraged further publication in *The Burlington Magazine* and contributions at the Design History Society Annual Conference in 1981 and the Association of Art Historians Annual Conference in 1984. Penny Sparke collaborated as joint author on an article for *Block* in 1986 entitled 'The Myth of the Independent Group' which forms the basis of Chapter Eight. Dorothy Morland, Director of the ICA throughout the 1950s has offered unfailing support. Thanks are also due to Lawrence Alloway, Mario Amaya, Mary Banham, Jane Drew, William Gear, James King, Dr Sarat Maharaj, Richard Morphet, Dr Christopher Mullen, Gillian Naylor, Eduardo Paolozzi, Dr Anthony Parton, Alison and Peter Smithson and Toni del Renzio for kindly offering useful help and information. Thanks to Vanessa Paynton, my Research Assistant, for the picture research. The opportunity to write the book came as part of my secondment as Reader at Southampton Institute – many thanks to my colleagues there, in particular those associated with the Research Centre for Consumer Culture, established in 1993 but inspired by the example of the Independent Group and their enthusiastic approach to design, mass culture and consumption.

# Introduction

THE MAJOR aim of this book is to offer a new understanding of the history of the Independent Group. To date, the Independent Group's significance has been assessed only within the broader history of Pop Art. This book offers a fresh analysis of the Group with reference to the meaning of modernism and mass culture in post-war Britain.

The term modernism in this context refers to the achievements of the European avant-garde in the early part of the twentieth century. Such developments in art and design enjoyed a limited degree of acceptance during the inter-war years amongst a particular circle of artists, designers and critics in Britain. During the 1930s modernism came to be increasingly identified with the left, with the rise of Fascism in Europe and the concurrent derision of 'Degenerate Art'.

Hitherto the Second World War has been represented in the history of British art as a watershed, dividing the European-orientated 1930s from the American-dominated 1950s. However, modernism was still a key issue in the 1940s and early 1950s in Britain. Discussion hinged on the notion that modernism was no longer relevant to post-war society and should be replaced by an indigenous school of painting and a national style in design. The climax of such efforts came with the Festival of Britain of 1951. As the scandal surrounding the purchase of William Gear's *Autumn Landscape* (1950) demonstrates, during 1951 modernism was still linked with the left. The founders of the Institute of Contemporary Arts (ICA) also made this connection and the Institute served as a flagship for the supposedly radical message of modernism during the late 1940s and early 1950s.

The Independent Group was a loose collection of artists, designers and writers whose careers had been impaired by war. Richard Hamilton, Eduardo Paolozzi, William Turnbull, Nigel Henderson, Peter Reyner, Mary Banham, and Alison and Peter Smithson gravitated towards the ICA as the only place in London where modern art and design could be seen and discussed. This group of young, disparate souls was bound together in their discussions, exhibitions and published writing by an admiration for Continental modernism. They only met officially between 1952 and 1955, but the problems they addressed and the solutions they offered inspired the subsequent work of all the members, and enjoys a special resonance today.

A distinction should be made at this point between the Independent Group's approach to modernism and that of the ICA management. The founders of the ICA, in particular Roland Penrose and Herbert Read, maintained that the role of the Institute should be to educate the public about the outstanding achievements of the European avant-garde – achievements which they never imagined could be surpassed. However, for the Independent Group, modernism acted as a starting point from which an analysis of culture was undertaken. Beginning from their varied social backgrounds and individual wartime experiences, the Group proposed a new, fresh approach to cultural analysis. From its foundation, the Independent Group began to construct its own analysis of culture by extending the perimeters of discussions on art and design to include references to new technology and non-Aristotelian philosophy.

From 1951 onwards the balance began to shift in the ideology of modernism at the ICA. The old, radical, European ICA began to disappear at the expense of a new, liberal, American-oriented ICA. This gradual change-over was certainly reflected in the second session of the Independent Group which focused almost exclusively on American culture. By 1956, when the Group had ceased to meet, modernism was identified with America, and Europe had relinquished leadership of the avant-garde.

Therefore, the history of the Independent Group is not explained within the terms of its influence on succeeding generations of artists, but is mapped out in relation to the changing ideology of modernism in Britain. Using this development as a reference point, a clearer understanding of the Independent Group is achieved. The critical framework which the Group constructed is then discussed in relation to developments in British Cultural Studies to argue for the enduring originality and relevance of their approach. My aim is to apply the illuminating approach of the Independent Group – with its reworking of modernism, erosion of the high/low culture divide and re-evaluation of consumption – to the history of the Group itself and its cultural context. The book ends with an analysis of the historiography of the Independent Group, examining its progress within the academic discourses of art history and cultural studies. The Group's intellectual achievements are then mapped against post-modernism and recent work on consumption.

# 1

# Welfare State culture

TO REACH a fuller understanding of the Independent Group the shifting pattern of the meaning of modernism in post-war Britain needs to be outlined. With the establishment of the Welfare State in Britain after the Second World War came the creation of a particular cultural ethos. Welfare State culture played an intrinsic part in the construction of a national identity during the late 1940s and 1950s. It drew on national tradition and succeeded in reworking pan-European modernism to represent this new national identity. It was this version of modernism against which the Institute of Contemporary Arts (ICA) and, in turn, the Independent Group, reacted.

The meanings of modernist culture in Britain before the Second World War were clear cut. Modernist culture was elitist. It excluded the masses by its very obscurity. Ironically, allegiances with left-wing politics were also a key feature of pre-war modernism. A radical position in relation to design was clearly articulated by the architectural critic John Summerson in 1945:

Hitler hates flat roofs. . . . But the trouble where Hitler is concerned is that the flat roof, the continuous horizontal window, the long unpillared span all coalesce under the sanction of a new philosophy of architecture, a philosophy identified with scientific thought, which is, in its very essence, anti-fascist and which Hitler intensely dislikes.[1]

Summerson was writing in the highly significant anthology, *This Changing World*. Edited by the British modernist sympathiser, J. R. M. Brumwell, the various contributors mapped out the part

which their own particular discipline would play in the restructur-
ing of British culture and society after the war. However, the tenor
of the collection of essays is largely determined by pre-war attitudes and allegiances. For the intelligentsia of the 1930s, left-wing
politics and modernism were synonymous. Radical art, for
example, in the case of *Unit One*, meant radical politics. For those
artists, designers and writers who had advocated modernism during
the 1930s, the post-war era seemed to offer a fantastic opportunity
to realise these ideals. With the advent of the first majority Labour
government in 1945, the attainment of a socialist utopia in Britain
seemed imminent. Modernist art and design critic Herbert Read
optimistically proclaimed in his contribution: 'But the individuals
in whom the spirit of modernism is embodied still survive, still
work, still create – however obscurely and intermittently. When the
cloud of war has passed, they will re-emerge eager to rebuild the
shattered world.'[2] However, Read's vision of a modernist
reconstruction of Britain by radical outsiders was never to become
a reality. The reason lay in Britain's weakening position on the
world stage coupled with America's ascendancy. Britain was shattered by the war and the period of reconstruction, which lasted well
into the 1950s created an atmosphere of insularity and xenophobia.
The national identity created by bodies such as the Ministry of
Information during the war continued to dominate official culture
and image making whilst the popularity of American mass culture,
established during the zenith of Hollywood, continued to flourish in
terms of advertising, television, music and film.

It was with reference to Britain's rural heritage and a fictional
community that an indigenous, national culture was constructed.
The notion that a small, rural community could act as both a para-
digm and an example for the nation at large was explored by Henry
Warren in his popular wartime novel, *England is a Village* (1941) and
by the films produced by Ealing studios. This vision of 'Little
England' detracted from the realities of living in ugly, bombed-out
cities. A glut of publications celebrated traditional British rural
crafts and ways of life. These included barge painting, tattooing,
circuses, gypsies, fairground decoration and patchwork quilts. The
texts celebrated the organic, community-based crafts of the pre-
industrial cottage dweller and denigrated contemporary, American
mass culture. The disappearance of folk art was rued by the various
authors as taste seemed to be imposed by the manufacturers
of mass-produced objects. As Barbara Jones argued in *The
Unsophisticated Arts* 'today, mass production makes its own traditional arts, inspired less and less by the consumers – I cannot believe

that there has been public clamour for streamlined perambulators or square clocks.'[3] Noel Carrington, in another volume of this genre, *Popular English Art*, deplored international modernism, likening it to the Renaissance for destroying the great English Gothic tradition. But the culture which was to be popular in Britain was not the indigenous type so favoured by middle-class commentators. It was the contemporary mass culture created in America which was to dominate the British popular imagination throughout the 1950s and which the Independent Group was to analyse. This was a period during which levels of disposable income rose and mass consumption became a reality in Britain (Figure 1).

This suspicion of pre-war modernism was characteristic of post-war British culture and society as a whole. With the establishment of the Welfare State, free health treatment and better education for all, the concept that art and design were part of the general prescription for the nation's health emerged. Paternalistic official bodies were founded to promote an appreciation of high culture which also celebrated the British national identity and appropriated elements of the international avant-garde. There was a widespread consensus of opinion among the various official bodies, partially because they had worked closely together under different titles during the war. One key example is the Council of Industrial Design (COID) which was founded in 1944 by the Board of Trade to raise the standard of British design by educating both the consumer and the manufacturer in the hope of increasing exports. Key figures on the new Council included Gordon Russell, the arts and crafts furniture maker and Josiah Wedgwood. The exhibition, *Britain Can Make It* was held at the Victoria and Albert Museum in 1946 and was the COID's first solo public venture. The aim was to continue the export drive as the new President of the Board of Trade, Sir Stafford Cripps, declared during a European Service broadcast on the eve of the exhibition's opening 'It is calculated that of the four hundred million pounds of goods exported before the war more than half were articles in which design played a large selling point.'[4] It was recognised that British design should be easily distinguished from the other major exporters of industrial design. The COID encouraged designers to combine British traditional design with modern, 'good' design – a message which had been part of the Board of Trade's propaganda throughout the war.

The reaction of visitors to the exhibition was recorded in a Mass Observation survey, which found 'The dominant trend is away from Utility. People are searching for something delicate and colourful, which will not remind them of wartime products.'[5] The

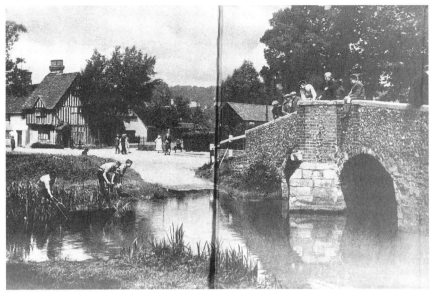

1] The frontispiece of a popular wartime publication, *Romantic Britain: The National Heritage of Beauty, History and Legend* (1944). Wartime nostalgia for a lost rural Britain was to inform the construction of a national identity after the Second World War

Contemporary Style was described by the Council in the fourth issue of *Design*. Contemporary did not necessarily mean 'geometrical, abstract, formal or Functional Designs,'[6] which the Council considered to be a minority taste. What was advocated was a style which accommodated such standards of British design as the Windsor chair and Harris tweed. Similarly, such traditional materials as wood, clay and pure new wool were not to be abandoned for newer inventions such as rayon, plywood and plastics. The Contemporary Style aimed to unite the best of past British design with a modern design look. The Council attempted to appeal to popular taste by launching the Contemporary Style for the Festival of Britain in 1951.

One source for the Contemporary was the traditional British archetype and the other was Scandinavian modernism. Perceived as warmer and more humane, with its reliance on soft woods, than German modernism, again Welfare State culture reworked the prewar connotations of modernism. An influential exhibition of *Danish Domestic Design* was organised by the Arts Council of Great Britain and the Council of Industrial Design in 1946. Furniture by Boerge Mogensen, kitchen equipment, textiles and tableware celebrated this organic, craft-orientated style. There was a parallel move in architecture with the popularity amongst British professionals for the New Empiricism, again based on Scandinavian forms. It was argued in the pages of *Architectural Review* that the Swedes had rejected objectivity and rationalism in architectural aesthetics, applying these qualities to the method of construction only. New Empiricism incorporated traditional materials, asymmetrical plans, pitched roofs and one-storey houses. Such humanistic architecture is indicative of the gentle Welfare State culture which permeated post-war Britain. Modernism was tempered by combining it with traditional forms and materials. There was a consensus of opinion amongst critics that high modernism had come to an end with the war and efforts should now be made to communicate with the public rather than foster the avant-garde.

The Arts Council of Great Britain certainly formed part of this consensus. Established as a Body Corporate in 1946, there was little difference between the Arts Council and its wartime predecessor, the Council for the Encouragement of Music and the Arts (CEMA) in structure and purpose. Limitations on the import of works of art in Britain continued until 1954, severely restricting what the Arts Council could exhibit. Exhibition space was in short supply after the war and the Council pursued the CEMA objective of promoting 'The Best for the Most'. As with the case of the Contemporary in design and the New Empiricism in architecture, a neologism emerged during the 1940s to describe an ethos in painting which the Arts Council supported and which acknowledged the debt to modernism, but drew heavily from traditional British sources. Neo-Romanticism ignored the formalist experiments of modernism and retracted into an approachable, humane and nationalistic style of painting.

The style had first emerged during the Second World War in the publicly commissioned work of John Piper, Graham Sutherland and Henry Moore. The term was introduced by Robin Ironside, then a wartime assistant at the Tate Gallery, London, in his essay *Painting Since 1939* written during 1945, published in pamphlet form by the British Council in 1946 and in book form with three other essays in 1948.[7] Ironside rightly argued that British artists were rejecting the European tenets of modernism as advocated by Roger Fry earlier in the century. Artists in Britain were returning to their native roots with a rediscovery of artists such as William Blake, Samuel Palmer and John Martin. The trend was toward illustration, lyricism and the British landscape. The movement flourished during the late 1940s and 1950s in the work of John Minton, Robert Colquhoun and Michael Ayrton. Moreover, Neo-Romanticism was the most widely represented style at the Arts Council's prestigious *60 for '51* exhibition at the Festival of Britain.

Through the arts and sciences, properly chosen and displayed, the 1951 Festival can demonstrate *British democracy in action*, past, present and future (with, of course, special emphasis on 1851–1951). By this means also, aided by full use of our incomparable rural and architectural heritage, we can rediscover the face of Britain to ourselves and to the world.[8]

This attempt to define the main purpose of the Festival of Britain came from its Executive Committee's Confidential Report of August 1948. From the planning stages, the Festival was intended to be a chauvinistic celebration of certain aspects of British culture. The 'face' which was rediscovered during 1951 and presented to the world was one of a nation revelling in the glories of past traditions, convinced of their perpetuation into a romantically-constructed future. The year 1951 was the time in which Neo-Romanticism, New Empiricism and the Contemporary reached the zenith of their influence and popular exposure (Figure 2).

**2]** Front cover, special issue of the *Illustrated London News*, 12 May 1951. A romantic evocation of the South Bank site featuring the Dome of Discovery and Skylon

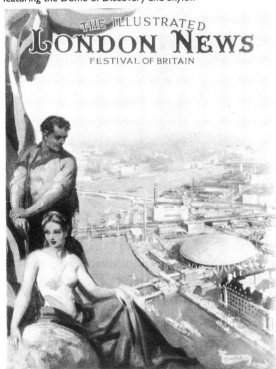

## Design at the Festival

Therefore, the Festival of Britain reinforced national identity. The structure of values was based on the national heritage, tradition, the rural rather than the industrial, individual enterprises rather than mass production and regionalism. These values were also celebrated in the painting, sculpture, architecture and design produced for the occasion.

A competition was run to select a corporate symbol for the Festival. The competition was restricted to eight designers, selected after consultation with the Arts Council and the Council of Industrial Design. The eight were: Milner Gray, Abram Games, Eckersley, Lee Elliott, Peter Ray, Hans Schleger, F. H. K. Henrion and Robin Day – the eight most prominent graphic designers in Britain at that time. In a brief sent to the invited designers it was stressed that the Festival would rejoice in the British way of life and 'It is hoped to springclean the face that Britain presents to the visitor from overseas.'[9] In June 1949 the Selection Committee decided upon the design of Abram Games, then a lecturer in design at the Royal College of Art, who was accustomed to designing within the patriotic idiom after spending five years as official poster design at the War Office, where he designed nearly one hundred posters. The symbol consisted of the head of Britannia surmounting a compass, draped with bunting and incorporating the date, 1951. This corporate symbol was utilised for all the official activities of the Festival and hence adorned letter-headings, posters and tickets. The symbol signified the national qualities which the organisers hoped the Festival would project. National tradition was highlighted with the use of the Britannia motif and the colour range most often used of red, white and blue. The string of pennants strung jauntily across the lower half of the compass denoted the apparent frivolity of the Festival. The inclusion of the compass indicated the projected nationwide appeal of the celebrations (Figure 3).

The theme of the lasting quality of national tradition was also reflected in the Council of Industrial Design's role in the Festival with regard to official style. The Council not only displayed and selected manufactured objects for the Festival, but also designated the official style as the Contemporary. To take one example, a small firm such as Robin and Dixon Nance from St. Ives successfully entered a handmade, ladder-back rocking-chair for exhibition. The chair, crafted from elm, ash and oak with seagrass seat was based on an eighteenth-century design. The Antelope Chair by Ernest Race

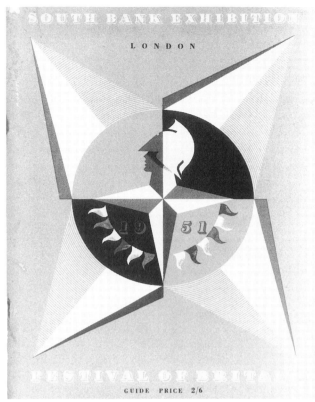

SOUTH BANK EXHIBITION

LONDON

1951

FESTIVAL OF BRITAIN

GUIDE PRICE 2/6

**3]** Official Guide for the Festival of Britain carrying Abram Games's prizewinning design for the emblem

and manufactured for use on the South Bank site exemplifies the Contemporary Style. Whilst the materials used and the skeletal form of the chair draw from modernist, Scandinavian design, the basic form of the chair derives from eighteenth-century British sources. The sphere and rod construction of the chair legs, so characteristic of 1950s' design, derived from the Council's introduction of the theme of molecular biology for the Festival Pattern Group. This consisted of twenty-eight British manufacturers who based textile prints, light-fittings, glass and ceramics on crystal diagrams. The notion of using crystal structures was inspired by Dr Kathleen Lonsdale's book on the subject, *Crystals and X-Rays*, published by G. Bell & Sons in 1948 and a paper read at Girton College Cambridge, in 1949. The paper analysed the structure of haemoglobin, polythene, beryl, cellulose, insulin and nylon. Hence, Festival designers such as Marianne Straub designed *Helmsley* for Warner & Sons Ltd based on the molecular structure of nylon. The crystal structure theme influenced not only flat design, but also three-

Welfare State culture

11

dimensional work. Edward Mill's design for a screen on the South Bank site appeared to be an enlarged scientific model of a molecular structure.

Therefore, the Council of Industrial Design made its first major impact on the general public with its extensive contribution to the Festival. As was also the case with architecture, an inoffensive and diluted form of modern design, which was also unmistakably British, was established as the norm. The major aims of the Festival, which were to acknowledge the achievements of the past and incorporate them into a vision of the future, were well represented by Festival design.

## Fine art at the Festival

Like the Council of Industrial Design, the Arts Council worked in close liaison with the Festival of Britain authorities, and was obliged to conform with Festival policies in its 1951 activities. Therefore, the Arts Council did not detract from its earlier practice of encouraging an indigenous style of painting in the form of Neo-Romanticism. However, there was one exception to this rule, when William Gear won a purchase prize in the *60 for '51* competition. The criticism which this work attracted from the press and public indicates the nature of the ideology of modernism in Britain in the early 1950s.

Decisions reached during the first full meeting of the Arts Council to discuss the Festival in 1947 certainly accorded with Festival policy: 'It was the unanimous view of the Council that the events organised for the Festival should represent the British arts only.'[10] Suggestions as to exactly how this should be implemented were slow to emerge. This was because the government took some time in deciding what the role of the Arts Council should be. Primarily, the government had designated a far more important role for the Arts Council in the Festival proceedings than it was eventually to play.[11] The decision was made in 1948 to hold the Festival of Britain on the South Bank site and the Arts Council's role diminished. The much reduced Festival of Arts took place in London during May and June of 1951. With an extra grant of £400,000 the Arts Council commissioned six operas and several orchestral works. The London season as a whole was planned to display British achievements. Featured composers included Purcell, Elgar and Benjamin Britten. Similarly, in the theatre Shakespeare and Shaw were highlighted. The role of the visual arts in the Festival came under extensive discussion, with various suggestions including a representation of the

British way of life, portraits of OBE winners or the suggestion of Sir Owen Morshead, Assistant Keeper of the Royal Archives, of composing a list of occupational types as commissions, for example: 'A postman, herring girl, game-keeper, piper of the Argyll and Sutherland Highlanders, a pearly King and a bluecoat boy.'[12] This was rejected by the Art Panel in October 1949 in the light of directives from the Festival Executive. Philip James, secretary of the Arts Council, received a letter from Gerald Barry 'in which he expressed the hope that the exhibition of British Contemporary Art should be shown in London during the main period of the Festival.'[13]

The possibility of showing contemporary British art had been discussed during August 1948, but the Panel had thought that this would be organised by the newly established Institute of Contemporary Arts (ICA). During a meeting of October 1949 the idea which was to become *60 for '51* was first aired by the Art Panel. The Panel recommended that five pictures be commissioned for £500 each, measuring not less than 40 by 50 inches. Panel members were then invited to submit suggestions for who the five should be but agreement could not be reached. The Art Panel therefore recommended that the Arts Council offer five prizes of £500 rather than commissions and that a limited number of painters be invited to enter a competition which would form an exhibition. Although the works were being commissioned five years after the war, materials were still in very short supply. Hence, one major incentive which the Arts Council offered was the supply of free canvas on which to paint. The reasoning behind the minimum dimensions of the paintings signifies two overall aims of the competition. Firstly, it seemed that this national celebration of all things British should be enhanced by a proclamation of the quality (and quantity) of British art. It was hoped that the monumental scale of the works produced would breathe an air of optimism into the rather exhausted world of British painting. The second justification offered by the Arts Council for the large-scale commissions, was that the exhibition should instigate the purchase of the paintings for public display by industry and the new public institutions created by the Welfare State. The organisers realised that patronage for the arts could no longer be left to the individual collector. As John Wren noted in his essay 'Bread and Circuses' in 1948:

in the capitalist era the creative artist fell on hard times through lack of patronage. This must not happen again in our democratic Socialist age; the people and the organisations representing the people must be the new patrons.[14]

Eventually only three of the fifty-four paintings shown were bought by the type of client at whom the show was aimed – a Miners' Welfare Institute, a church and a comprehensive school. Four of the paintings remain untraced and twenty-two are housed in public collections.

The three judges met on 16 April 1951 to select the five prize-winners. They were: the art critic for *The Times*, Alan Clutton-Brock, Jonkheer Sandberg, Director of the Stedelijk Museum, Amsterdam and A. J. L. McDonell, Adviser to the Felton Bequest, National Gallery of Victoria, Australia. The decision arrived at by the judges was validated by the Arts Council two days later and announced in *The Times* on 21 April. The fifty-four paintings finally went on public view on 2 May at Manchester City Art Gallery. This initial opening venue was in keeping with the Festival's aim of involving the public on a regional basis. The exhibition toured eleven regional galleries from Plymouth to Newcastle, showing at the New Burlington Galleries, Suffolk Street, London during June.

The major problem which the show presented for the Arts Council was the controversy which the choice of prize-winners caused among the public. As early as 10 April 1951 Kenneth Clark had stated at an Art Panel meeting of the Arts Council that the Panel should have made the selection of purchase prize-winners. Four of the selections attracted little comment. Claude Rogers's *Miss Lynn* was perhaps the least innovative of prize-winners. This safe, academic painting in the mould of Manet's *Olympia* was painted when Rogers was on the staff of the Slade School of Art. Two other members of staff were also amongst the prize-winners. These were Robert Medley's *Bicyclists Against a Blue Background* and Lucien Freud's *Interior Near Paddington*. The gigantic *Aquarian Nativity – Child of This Age* by Ivon Hitchens was also a prize-winner, a precursor of later murals such as that executed for the English Folk Dance and Song Society in 1954, which measured 21 by 6 metres.

However, it was the fifth of the prize-winners, William Gear's *Autumn Landscape* (Figure 4) which attracted an extremely hostile response from press and public alike. Most vitriolic was the *Daily Mail* which printed a reproduction of *Autumn Landscape* on the front page of its 19 April issue and asked 'What price Autumn on Canvas?' It appeared that it was the price paid for the painting which was most objectionable. The *Daily Mail* emphasised that the £500 came from government funds. The *Daily Telegraph* of the same date carried a reproduction of the painting with a similar story. This instigated a two-month-long debate in the letter pages of the

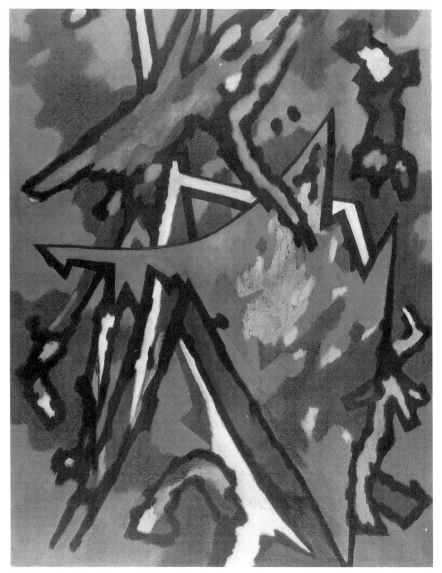

**4]** William Gear, *Autumn Landscape* (1950). Oil on canvas, 183 × 127 cm. Laing Art Gallery, Newcastle. The abstract canvas which caused a furore of controversy during the Festival year

*Daily Telegraph*. Not only was the cost of purchase discussed, but also the modern nature of Gear's painting. William G. Luscombe's letter appeared on 21 April 1951 and is typical of many:

Nature's beauty and man's abstractions of ugliness are far apart. To praise the latter seems humbug. If any Art Council or committee truly cared for and respected great traditions in all branches of the fine arts they would, instead of purchasing, condemn such fooleries as are now applauded, encouraged and advertised.

Criticisms of Gear's painting tended to identify it as an example of ugly, modern art in contrast to the beauty of traditional painting. The painting's political meaning came to light when traditional, established painters voiced their discontent over the affair. Complaints were made against the Arts Council by a lobby of painters upon the announcement of the sixty invited artists in January 1951. The painters formed an *ad hoc* committee, and included Augustus John, William Russell Flint, Dame Laura Knight and Gerald Moira. The committee complained that the Arts Council was partisan and 'leaning too far to the left.'[15] Therefore, traditional artists were making the same correlation between radical art and radical politics which Herbert Read and others had been making since the 1930s. William Gear himself replied to criticisms made of his work in the *Daily Telegraph* warning that the public should not be afraid of being labelled 'Bolshie' as a penalty for appreciating his work.[16] Public opinion was running at such a pitch that on 3 May the Liberal MP for Eye, Edgar Granville, was compelled to put a question on the subject to the Chancellor of the Exchequer. Granville's major objection seemed to be that the painting was 'not representative of British art,'[17] and he queried who had been consulted about the purchase. Hugh Gaitskell, in a written reply by Philip James, stated:

I am aware that one of the five pictures recently purchased by the Arts Council has been criticised in some newspapers which could, of course, print only a small black and white photograph of it. I am assured that, taken together, these pictures are widely representative in style and cover various aspects of contemporary British painting.[18]

Gaitskell's statement was subtly in agreement with Granville's objection: by taking the prize-winners as an entire group the provocative nature of Gear's work was not refuted. The debate continued throughout 1951 as the Arts Council received letters of complaint and by the end of the *60 for '51* in 1952, *Autumn Landscape* was the sole prize-winner not to have entered a public collection. What made the Gear painting so unpopular?

From the letters of complaint it was the international, modern nature of the work which so many found objectionable. The exhibition attempted to integrate Festival of Britain policy with that of the Arts Council by promoting wholly British culture. None of the contributing artists had spent as much time abroad as Gear had done. Gear had returned to Britain only during 1950 after spending three years painting and exhibiting in Paris and had not assimilated the influence of Neo-Romanticism. The majority of the paintings in *60 for '51* could be described as Neo-Romantic – predominantly lyrical, inoffensive with a recognisable subject, usually landscape. Gear's painting was uncompromising, aggressive and abstract. During the three years which Gear spent in Paris he made contact with the artists of *L'Ecole de Paris* and consolidated his abstract style. Paintings produced since 1947 confirm the importance that contact with artists such as Nicholas de Staël, Hans Hartung, Pierre Soulages and Alfred Manessier had for Gear. It was the foreign nature of Gear's work which distinguished it from most of the other exhibits and which countered the consensus of Welfare State culture. The Festival of Britain presented a specific image of Britain, both to the indigenous population and to visitors from abroad. The 'face of Britain' in 1951 depended largely for its security on traditional values of the past to cope with the future. The monarchy, the hard-working British people and the bonds of a strong community spirit were all facets of the British way of life which the Festival sought to emphasise. Festival art and design was symptomatic of these tendencies. Appropriate styles in art and design, were reworked from Britain's past. This trend dominated British culture during the first ten years after the war, and may partly explain the apparent unpopularity of the ICA in their single-minded promotion of European modernism.

## Notes

1 J. Summerson, 'New Groundwork of Architecture' in J. R. M. Brumwell (ed.), *This Changing World*, Readers Union/George Routledge & Sons, 1945, p. 182.

2 H. Read, 'Threshold of a New Age' in *This Changing World*, 1945, p. 12.

3 B. Jones, *The Unsophisticated Arts*, Architectural Press, 1951, p. 9.

4 *The Times*, 25 September 1946, p. 2.

5 Unpublished survey by Mass Observation, commissioned by COID, 1946, p. 9, Design Council Archives.

6 *Design*, No. 4, April 1949, p. 1.

7 *Since 1939*, Longmans, Green & Co. Ltd (1948) included Arnold L. Haskell on 'Ballet Since 1939', Dilys Powell on 'Films Since 1939', Rollo Myers on 'Music Since 1939' and Robin Ironside on 'Painting Since 1939'. As the four essays were originally commissioned by the British Council it is unsurprising that they emphasised national achievements in the arts and encouraged those involved to counter foreign competition.

8 The Festival Executive Committee, Confidential Report, *Festival of Britain: Purpose and Approach to Theme*, 1948, p. 1, Design Council Archives.

9 Brief circulated to the designers invited to submit for the Festival symbol competition from the Executive Committee, p. 1, Design Council Archives.

10 Minutes of the Meeting of the Arts Council, 27 February 1948, p. 3, Arts Council Archives.

11 Minutes of the Meeting of the Arts Council, 29 January 1947, p. 1, Arts Council Archives.

12 Minutes of the Meeting of the Arts Council Executive Committee, 7 September 1949, p. 1, Arts Council Archives.

13 Minutes of the Meeting of the Art Panel, Arts Council, 12 April 1949, p. 2, Arts Council Archives.

14 John Wren 'Bread and Circuses', *Tribune*, 20 February 1948.

15 The *Daily Telegraph*, 10 August 1951, p. 3.

16 W. Gear, 'Criticism Without Knowledge', The *Daily Telegraph*, 26 April 1951.

17 *The Times*, 4 May 1951, p. 4.

18 *Ibid*.

# 2

# Modernism and the ICA

THE FOUNDING and early history of the Institute of Contemporary Arts (ICA) represents an important moment for modernism in Britain. The Arts Council reinforced the creation of a consensus in post-war Britain by combining an indigenous style of painting with modernism which accorded with the aims of parallel bodies like the COID. The ICA pursued a more elitist and purist route by promoting European modernism in Britain, a route which met with little public sympathy or understanding but which galvanised the post-war British art and design scene. Events and exhibitions staged by the Institute during the early post-war years provide an exciting insight into avant-garde culture. This explains why future members of the Independent Group gravitated towards the Institute. As the history of the ICA is yet to be written and the foundation laid during the late 1940s was so critical for the Independent Group and has subsequently been neglected, this chapter will chart the Institute's beginnings. The Institute of Contemporary Arts provided much more than a meeting-place for the Independent Group: it was integral to its formation and pro-vided a crucial stimulus for its discussions.

The critical stance of the ICA was determined by the founding Organising Committee and their pre-war contacts and activities in the world of international modernism. Roland Penrose, Herbert Read and E. L. T Mesens were the three signatories of the letter, dated 22 January 1946, which called those who were interested in establishing a Museum of Modern Art to a meeting at the London Gallery, Brook Street. According to Penrose, the ICA began with the International Surrealist Exhibition at the New Burlington Galleries in 1936.[1] Penrose had been living in Paris since his graduation from Queens' College, Cambridge in 1922 and was close to avant-garde developments in France, particularly Surrealism. A chance meeting with an English poet and advocate of Surrealism, David Gascoyne, in Paris during 1935 led to the formation of an English pocket of Surrealists and the New Burlington Galleries exhibition. One leading member of the group was Herbert Read, who was the champion of modernism in Britain and acted as *Unit One*'s apologist in 1934. During the 1930s Read had published extensively on modernism in art and design including *Art Now: An Introduction to the Theory of Modern Painting and Sculpture* in 1933 and *Art and Industry: The Principles of Industrial Design* in 1934. These two books formed the most incisive works in English on modernism. The linchpin of his cultural theory was that there was a Neo-Platonic essence to all 'good' art and design ranging from palaeolithic times to abstract painting. There was also a streak of anarchy in Read's work, which he acknowledged in an interview in 1946 to mark the founding of the ICA. Always a dedicated admirer of Jung, he believed that everyone has innate artistic ability which is waiting to be unleashed. For Read it is society which hampers such creative expression. Read was uncomfortable with the new, majority Labour government's commandeering of culture. Writing in 1947 to Naum Gabo he declared that England had become 'completely finished because now based on assumptions which deprive social life of incentive. . . . I begin to think that the Americans are right to keep to a capitalist economy until a better alternative than state socialism becomes evident.'[2]

The third signatory of the 1946 letter was E. L. T. Mesens, a Belgian Surrealist and close friend of René Magritte. Mesens visited London to assist with the hanging and organisation of the International Surrealist exhibition, settled there subsequently and ran the London Gallery in Cork Street. The London Gallery provided the central focus for Surrealist events in Britain, and several precedents for the ICA were set. These included the publication of a Bulletin, the exhibition policy of showing leading modernist artists from mainland Europe and mixed exhibitions on Surrealist themes. Penrose and Mesens remained committed to the Surrealist movement throughout the 1930s and 1940s. However, Herbert Read's affinities were always more heterogeneous, supporting the avant-garde as a whole rather than Surrealism in particular. That such a difference of opinion did not prevent the three from working together indicated something of the character of British

Surrealism. Part of the explanation lies in the lack of a Dada movement in Britain, indeed the Independent Group was later to identify itself with Dada as a criticism of the ICA management.

Before the war, discussion took place around the subject of establishing a modern art centre in London. These suggestions were reviewed at the first meeting of the Museum of Modern Art Organising Committee on 30 January 1946. Present at the meeting apart from the three convenors were four other Surrealist sympathisers. One was Peter Watson, the wealthy collector who had financed the launch of the literary magazine *Horizon* and lived in Paris during the 1930s. (He drove a Bentley with leopard-skin upholstery and had visited America with Salvador Dalí.) Experimental film-maker Jacques Brunius, and G. M. Hoellering, who ran the Academy Cinema in Oxford Street, represented film at the first meeting. The final member was E. C. (Peter) Gregory who had mixed in Surrealist circles before the war and who chaired the printing firm of Lund Humphries and was a director of the *Burlington Magazine*. The meeting reviewed previous schemes for establishing a modern art centre in London. The *Circle* group of artists' plans for establishing a Museum of Living Art under Read were thought to have been dropped in 1938. The notion of establishing a contemporary art centre under the patronage of Peggy Guggenheim had also been discussed before the war, with the proposal that Read act as adviser. Following the war Guggenheim had become involved with her project in Venice. However, a letter from her to Roland Penrose suggests that he had been rather hasty in presuming that she had no further interest in the London project. 'The day before I got your letter I decided to send you the minimum modest sum of £100. Sorry to disappoint you but I can't do £1000 now as you had hoped. I have my own baby here – to console me for the one you stole in London.'[3]

The Organising Committee was convinced of the need to establish a contemporary art centre in the bleak economic climate of postwar London which would be international, which would encourage younger, unknown artists and which would cater for a broad spectrum of the arts. The source of such ideals lay not only in the Surrealist movement, but also in New York's Museum of Modern Art. Indeed, the Organising Committee's first working title was the 'Museum of Modern Arts Scheme', which was supplanted by the 'Institute of Contemporary Arts' in May 1946. Because the founder members of the ICA placed such an emphasis on a multidisciplinary approach to culture, four new members were included for the second meeting, held on 20 February 1946. Edward Clark accepted Peter

Watson's invitation to join the Committee as a representative of avant-garde music. J. M. Richards attended the second meeting as the architectural expert. Two art critics, sensitive to the aims of Surrealism also attended; they were Douglas Cooper, and Robert Melville who had worked at the London Gallery and then ran the Hanover Gallery from 1948.

This powerful, all-male team met monthly and the minutes of their meetings indicate the lively nature of their deliberations. Surrealist humour was certainly in evidence when, during the very first meeting, twelve Herbert Reads were voted on to the Preparatory Committee. The more serious points of discussion during the 1946 to 1948 meetings, that of finance and premises, had to wait until much later to be resolved. The first task which faced the Organising Committee was to produce a public statement which summarised the aims of the ICA, an exercise initially assigned to Douglas Cooper. However, his first and second drafts of the Statement of Policy were unanimously rejected by the Committee as being too inflammatory. Cooper stressed the radical public image of modernism and claimed that existing institutions favoured only the accepted and the dead. In a letter to Herbert Read he argued: 'What one should do is make the Tate, CEMA and the British Council look as silly as they are – and this does not mean compromise, but making modern things clear to the ordinary person by giving them the necessary fodder.'[4] However, the ICA's founders were no longer young rebels and sought some degree of public acceptance for the project. The Arts Council and the COID had attempted to integrate a toned down modernism with traditional British style. This hesitant acceptance of modernism by official bodies accorded it more respectability. Therefore, figures like Read and Penrose were no longer operating as outsiders in British culture. For example, Herbert Read was knighted in 1953 and joined the Fine Arts Committee of the British Council in 1941 and remained a member until 1967, taking a leading role in the selection of artists for the Venice Biennale and for the purchase of contemporary art. Therefore, the aim was to work with and not against the Arts Council and the Tate Gallery. Cooper resigned from the Organising Committee over this issue and characteristically conducted a personal vendetta against the ICA throughout the late 1940s. Cooper's campaign was pursued so vigorously that legal action was considered by the Committee after he had warned the fine art dealer Freddy Mayor against lending works to ICA exhibitions.

The existence of the ICA initially came to the attention of the public through a letter to *The Times* from Herbert Read on 26 June 1947. The letter outlined the aims of the new Institute and invited those who were interested to send for copies of the Statement of Policy, which Read had rewritten. The initial response was positive, with over three hundred requests for the Statement. In authentic Surrealist style, the ICA first attracted widespread public attention and notoriety through a controversial exhibition. *Forty Years of Modern Art: 1907–1947. A Selection from British Collections* was held from 9 February to 6 March 1948 in George Hoellering's Academy Hall in Oxford Street (Figure 5). It is entirely representative of the early ICA that its first exhibition should be a celebration of the European avant-garde with Surrealism enjoying the spotlight. Just as the Museum of Modern Art exhibitions and collection in New York displayed the taste and wealth of its patrons, so *Forty Years of Modern Art* drew extensively from the collections of the Organising Committee.[5]

The painting and sculpture sub-committee of the ICA which consisted of Penrose, Melville and Mesens, compiled an initial list of

**5]** Front cover of the exhibition catalogue for *Forty Years of Modern Art*

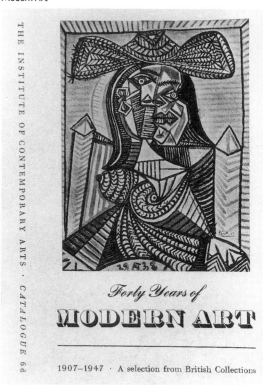

THE INSTITUTE OF CONTEMPORARY ARTS · CATALOGUE 6d

*Forty Years of*

## MODERN ART

1907–1947 · A selection from British Collections

artists for the exhibition. This was then criticised by the full Committee for not including sufficient young, unknown artists, as one of the principal aims of the Institute was to foster new art. This was rectified by adding the names of Robert Colquhoun, Robert MacBryde, Lucien Freud, John Craxton and Eduardo Paolozzi. The latter is one of the earliest records of a future member of the Independent Group contributing to an ICA event. Paolozzi's work *Fisherman and Wife* (Figure 6) had been bought from the Mayor Gallery by Gregory in December 1947, probably for the exhibition,

**6**] Eduardo Paolozzi, *Fisherman and Wife* (1946, Tate Gallery). Collage made from Indian ink and coloured paper. 76.8 × 61 cm. Bought from the Mayor Gallery by E. C. Gregory in December 1947. Purchased from the executors of the late E. C. Gregory with grant aid by the Tate Gallery in 1959

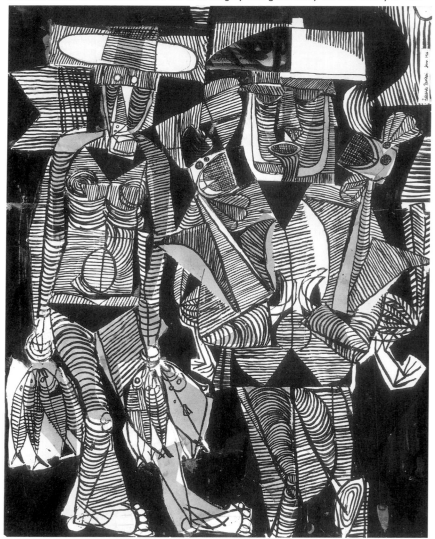

where it was exhibited as *Two Figures*. The exhibition provided a comprehensive overview of twentieth-century, European avant-garde painting and sculpture. The 127 exhibits included five Picassos, three Braques, three Matisses and Surrealist work by Dalí, de Chirico and Magritte first seen at the 1936 Surrealist show. The exhibition enjoyed moderate critical success in the art press and was gently ridiculed by the popular newspapers, many of which carried a photograph of the F. E. McWilliam Surrealist nude which stood outside the Academy Halls, with various captions ranging from 'Oh Dear! Is This Another New Look?' to 'You Never Know What's Waiting For You Round the Corner'.[5] This was the type of public reaction which the Arts Council could not risk eliciting itself but which the ICA deliberately attracted. Therefore the Arts Council made an early grant to the ICA for general purposes, not specifically for mounting the exhibition, to avert any unwelcome publicity. This established a working pattern which has continued until the present day – the ICA being a conduit for extreme exhibitions or events which the Arts Council could not directly foster themselves. As Philip James acknowledged in 1951: 'they not only arrange their own exhibitions, many of which relieve the Arts Council of a certain responsibility, especially in the field of avant-garde art.'[6]

The ICA had decided to approach the Arts Council for funds in a meeting of 29 April 1947 and the Art Director, Philip James, had secured the support of Sir Kenneth Clark on a train journey to Scotland. Further support was forthcoming for the ICA's next exhibition, *40,000 Years of Modern Art* which was staged in the Academy cinema basement from 21 December 1948 to 29 January 1949 (Figure 7). Again the Arts Council awarded a grant of £500 to mount the show. The exhibition was conceived by Herbert Read and sought to illustrate one of the prevailing themes of his writing, that there is a marked similarity between modern art and non-western art from earlier periods. As he explained at the press conference prior to the opening of the show:

The art of primitive people is no longer to us merely a manifestation of the disgusting idol worship of savages and cannibals. We have discovered in it powers of invention and expression which fill us with amazement and seem to point the way to new forms of art which can combine primitive vitality and vision with modern technique and sensibility . . . And one of the strange facts that emerges is that some of the earliest exhibits particularly the mammoth ivory Venus from the caves of the Dordogne (which it seems is a good 40,000 years old) appears to be the most modern in conception.[7]

Such white, male, western attitudes to the art of the 'other' was a founding principle of modernism and one which found currency at

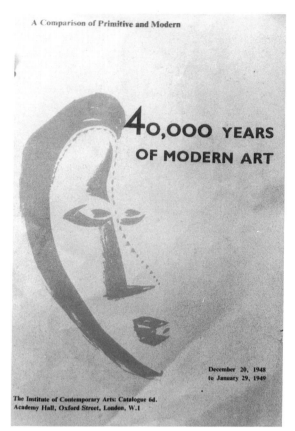

**4**0,000 YEARS
OF MODERN ART

December 20, 1948
to January 29, 1949

The Institute of Contemporary Arts: Catalogue 6d.
Academy Hall, Oxford Street, London, W.1

**7]** Front cover of the exhibition catalogue for *40,000 Years of Modern Art*

the ICA. In particular Read wished to demonstrate the similarity between naive modern art and the imagined raw power of the unsophisticated 'primitive'. This idea found little favour with the curators of the Ashmolean Museum Oxford who lent a Cycladic Venus but refused permission to feature it on a poster for the exhibition as it was to be juxtaposed with a Giacometti nude. A major scoop for the exhibition was the inclusion of Picasso's *Les Demoiselles d'Avignon* (1906–7) for an insurance fee of $330, borrowed from the Museum of Modern Art, New York (Figure 8). The work was loaned on the strength of goodwill built up by Penrose when he lent important works from his collection to the Museum during the war.

Not only did the Arts Council directly fund certain exhibitions for the ICA, but the two bodies also collaborated on shows. The display of *Modern German Prints and Drawings* at the Arts Council's St James's Square Gallery during November 1949 was a joint venture.

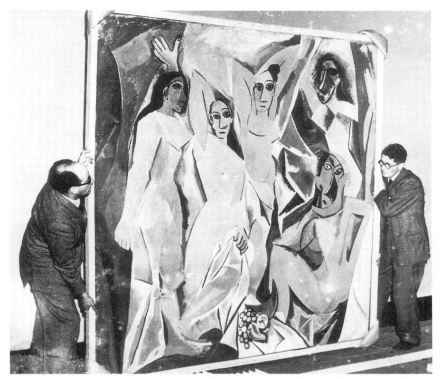

8] Ewan Phillips, then Director of the ICA, and Roland Penrose to the right, hanging Picasso's *Demoiselles d'Avignon* in the second ICA exhibition, *40,000 Years of Modern Art* in 1949

Works by German Expressionists such as Käthe Kollwitz, Karl Schmidt-Rottluff and Ernst Ludwig Kirchner received a rare English showing. It is indicative of the esteem in which the Arts Council held the ICA that in their Art Panel meeting held to discuss the Festival of Britain the possibility of the ICA organising the showing of contemporary British art for the Festival was considered. The Arts Council later approved the ICA's plans for *Ten Decades of British Taste* with a grant of £1,500. The ICA was restricted to British art for their Festival show and could not show contemporary British art, as this would clash with *60 for '51*. Thus they organised their only purely historical, British exhibition.

This critical review of British taste featured a selection of paintings from 1851–1951 which were popular in their day, displayed alongside contemporary criticism. This included Whistler's *Nocturne* (1877) with the infamous Ruskin text. Although Geoffrey Grigson stressed in the catalogue that the object of the exhibition was not to poke fun at British taste, the show could hardly be interpreted as doing anything else. *The Times* critic noted that the exhibition resembled 'nothing so much as a large provincial art gallery the suc-

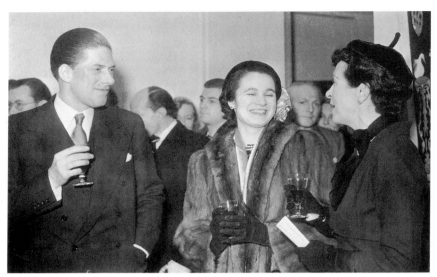

**9]** The official opening of the ICA on 12 December 1950. Earl and Countess Harewood enjoy a drink with Margaret Rawlings (Lady Barlow)

cessive directors of which have not been allowed to relegate any of their predecessors' purchases to the cellars.'[8] The Arts Council also enabled the ICA to purchase their first premises in Dover Street in the West End of London in 1950. The official opening of the premises by Lord Harewood on 12 December 1950 confirmed the view that the ICA was the place to go for outrageous art (Figure 9). The *Evening Standard* christened the premises the 'Advanced Guard H.Q.'[9] and continued 'The place has been reconstructed and redecorated in a manner that is uncompromisingly "contemporary".' The Dover Street offices, bar and gallery were refurbished under the direction of architect Jane Drew, curtain fabrics were designed by the young Terence Conran and the furniture by Neil Morris and Ernest Race. The opening exhibition, *1950: Aspects of British Art*, included work by Paolozzi, Hamilton and Turnbull as well as other young, avant-garde British artists (Figure 10). By 1951 the ICA had definitely acquired a certain image. The *Glasgow Herald* reported on 'The too-too arty air of the Institute of Contemporary Arts has often an unhappy effect on anything shown there, infecting quite blameless matters with the contagion of hi-falutin' nonsense.'[10] Dorothy Morland, the Director of the ICA throughout the 1950s admitted 'We are often accused of being a "clique", a cliché term which is hard to refute. Any small, closely knit organisation which depends on enthusiasm and dedication is bound to have elements of so-called "clique" to hold it together.'[11] Morland defended the Institute's elitism by declaring its intention to avoid mediocrity.

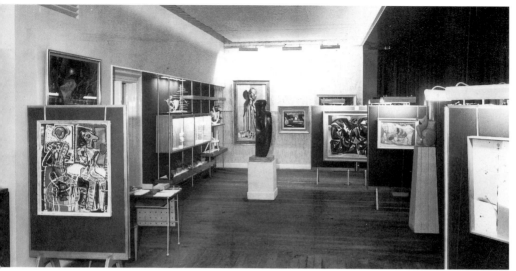

10] Installation shot, *1950: Aspects of British Art* held in the ICA's cramped Dover Street premises in December 1950. Work by Richard Hamilton to the right and sculpture by William Turnbull and Eduardo Paolozzi in the cabinet to the rear

Throughout the 1950s the ICA organised an impressive array of exhibitions and events which fed into Independent Group activities. During the Festival of Britain year, when patriotic celebrations of national culture were at their height, the ICA showed work by Matta and Picasso as well as Surrealist films, including *Un Chien Andalou* and *The Seashell and the Clergyman*. From December 1950 and throughout 1951 a series of *Public Views* were held which were concerned with the discussion of contemporary exhibitions. Richard Hamilton and Eduardo Paolozzi contributed towards the second *Public View*, chaired by David Sylvester, which took place in Dover Street on 9 January 1951. The subject of this discussion was the work of an Italian primitive, Orneore Metelli then on show at the Hanover Gallery. The discussion of Metelli's paintings centred on whether such unsophisticated work could be considered art at all. Matvyn Wright, Patrick Heron and Eric Newton doubted whether such technically incompetent work was art. In Wright's opening remarks he made his opinion clear:

He felt that a painter such as Metelli was easily placed in a cult centring on the adoration of the child at the present time . . . . Now we were invited to look at his pictures as we might look at a work by Michelangelo . . . I think him an incompetent bungler and an amateur.[12]

Because the precepts of modernism were largely being abandoned by many British artists and critics at this time, it is not surprising that such a view of primitivism was expressed at the discussion. It is equally unsurprising to find Roland Penrose and his wife, Lee Miller, defending the naive painter. Paolozzi too acknowledged the debt of modernism in appreciating such work: 'it is one of the revolutions of the past 40 or 50 years that we now could see the works of unprofessional painters – madmen, children, primitives. I think Metelli gets it across.'[13] However, as was to be the case with the Independent Group's approach to modernism, Paolozzi acknowledged the legacy of modernist art, but attempted to move on to a new assessment of the problem: 'everybody was using the arguments of the 1890s. The only point was, was Metelli as good as Vivin, Bombois and Co.? Was he a good primitive? That was the only point.'[14] The discussion of Pasmore's work hinged on the conscious and unconscious intentions of the artist. Pasmore was then teaching at the Central School of Arts and Crafts, where Hamilton was also to work after finishing at the Slade School of Art, London, and from which point they were to develop a basic design course. However, it becomes clear from this discussion that the two artists were not yet close associates. During the discussion Pasmore expressed the view that he took an empirical approach to his work. Hamilton disagreed, as he works as a rational, intellectual painter who plans the result of a picture before he begins.[15] Therefore, the programme of discussions organised by the ICA provided a platform on which disparate views on contemporary art and design could be compared. The discussions contributed towards the Independent Group's basic understanding of modernism and enabled them to hear and question the views held by many leading critics and historians.

Britain hosted the Tenth Congrès Internationaux d'Architecture Moderne (CIAM) Congress in 1951 and the opportunity to hear the views of eminent modern architects in London for the event was not missed by the ICA. This led to design and architecture contributing more to the ICA's programme than it had previously. Le Corbusier opened the *Growth and Form* exhibition on 3 July. His opening remarks were flattering of Hamilton, although his interpretation of the exhibition tended to stress the everlasting, universal laws of nature: 'This rich new vocabulary provides a good means for the discovery of the visible and the invisible universe; it allows the best in art to find all the new forms of these natural conceptions and harmonies, and to lift the spirit by poetical needs.'[16] Philip Johnson lectured at the ICA on 'Modern Architecture' and Serge Chermayeff on 'Education for Designers' in July 1951. The lecture programme at the ICA throughout 1950 and 1951 featured many important figures for European modernism speaking on various topics pertinent to the avant-garde. Sybil Moholy-Nagy talked on the work of her husband; Maxwell Fry on 'Modern Architecture' and Paul Eluard on Picasso. Concurrently Dr J. P. Hodin ran a course of lectures on contemporary art. It would be safe to assume that the future Independent Group members who were by this stage involved with ICA exhibitions, would have also attended a selection of the ICA lectures, hence augmenting their knowledge of modernism.

Apart from *Growth and Form*, the exhibition programme for 1951 reflected conventional ICA management tastes. Graham Sutherland was given a retrospective and Picasso's seventieth birthday was celebrated with an exhibition. Paolozzi, Turnbull and Hamilton exhibited again within the auspices of the ICA in the foyer of the Warner Theatre, Leicester Square London during June. Paolozzi showed *Study for the Cage* (1951, plaster on wire) the maquette for his Festival of Britain contribution. Also on show by Paolozzi was *Forms on a Bow* (1951, welded steel) not the version which he had shown at the ICA in 1950, but the same bow form decorated with curved steel rods. Turnbull showed one sculpture, *Caged Bird* (1950, copper) an angular, linear piece reminiscent of Klee. Hamilton exhibited two subtle, abstract canvases based on his *Growth and Form* work, *Microcosmos (Chromatic Spiral)* and *Microcosmos (Induction)* both of 1950.

Therefore, by the ICA Director's own admission, the Institute was an elitist organisation – a lonely outpost for avant-garde experiment in dour post-war Britain. Membership during the early 1950s wavered between one and two thousand. The ICA attempted to promote the values of the European avant-garde in the xenophobic atmosphere of Festival of Britain London. Although the role of the ICA is never mentioned in existing accounts of the Independent Group, the way in which the Institute advocated the cause of modernism partly determined the nature of the Group. Not only did the ICA provide a critical platform for the Group, many of the issues which the group concerned itself with had precedents in earlier ICA activities.

## Notes

1  Roland Penrose in interview with author, 29 September 1983.
2  Unpublished MS dated 28 February 1947, Yale University Library.
3  Unpublished MS dated 1 November 1947, ICA Archives.
4  Unpublished MS dated 22 February 1946, ICA Archives.

5 *Shields Evening News*, 10 February 1948, p. 8 and the *Evening Standard*, 9 February 1948, p. 5.

6 P. James, Arts Council Paper 298, 19 February 1951.

7 Unpublished transcript of Herbert Read's press conference speech, undated, p. 2, ICA Archives.

8 *The Times*, 15 August 1951, p. 8.

9 The *Evening Standard*, 6 December 1950, p. 5.

10 The *Glasgow Herald*, 12 April 1951, p. 3.

11 Dorothy Morland's unpublished memoirs, p. 18, ICA Archives.

12 Transcription of Public View No. 1, 9 January 1951, p. 1, ICA Archives.

13 Transcription of Public View No. 1, 1951, p. 2.

14 Transcription of Public View No. 1, pp. 10–11.

15 The following dialogue between the two painters elucidates the difference between their approaches: 'Hamilton: Does a concept ever suggest a painting? Pasmore: Yes, the concept of a spiral could start a picture. Hamilton: It means no more to you than that? Pasmore: No. (He then left the meeting.)' *Ibid*.

16 Le Corbusier, Opening Remarks on *Growth and Form* exhibition, 3 July 1951, p. 2.

# 3

## *Growth and Form*: the founding of the Independent Group

BECAUSE THE Independent Group has traditionally been explained as the Fathers of Pop, the precedents for the members' own work and the reasons for its formation have been neglected in art history.[1] The overarching enthusiasm which led to the formation of the Independent Group was modernism. Whilst existing accounts of the Group emphasise the similarity of class background and age, none dwells on the Group's enduring admiration for modern art, architecture and design. What is interesting in the context of Read's enthusiasm for the Bauhaus and Surrealism is that the Independent Group deconstructed modernist design theory and re-evaluated the work of the Dadaists. Recent post-modernist theory has tended to treat modernism as a homogeneous whole. However, during the creation of the modern movement and in the early post-war years there were many warring factions – even within each movement. These young artists, architects and writers who were to form the Independent Group came to modernism fresh from their wartime experiences and extracted an entirely different meaning from that of the British pre-war Surrealists and post-war Welfare State worthies. Inspired by the philosophy of logical positivism and existentialism, the Group arrived at a new understanding of modernism which emphasised the history of science and technology and gloried in the disorder of human existence as opposed to the preciousness of metaphysical art.

The historiography of the Independent Group stresses that it was the provincial, working-class roots of the members which provided the initial common ground for the Group's activities. However, it was the Slade School of Art in London which formed the initial meeting-place for the four most prominent practising artists in the Group. Moreover, it was an interest in modernism rather than their social origins which cemented their friendship. A close analysis of the backgrounds of Eduardo Paolozzi, Nigel Henderson, William Turnbull and Richard Hamilton reveals that none of the four hailed from the working class. Indeed, the privileged background of at least one member, Nigel Henderson, led directly to his personal understanding of modernism. His mother, Wyn Henderson, managed Nancy Cunard's Hours Press in Paris surrounded by Surrealist originals.[2] After quarrelling with Cunard, Wyn Henderson returned to London to live in the heart of Bloomsbury in Gordon Square. Nigel on one of his frequent visits saw an early performance of Virginia Woolf's *Freshwater* in Vanessa Bell's studio and stayed with Bell and Duncan Grant at Charleston. During a trip to the south of France in 1932 Nigel Henderson was introduced to Max Ernst who inspired his decision to become a fine artist. Back in London Wyn Henderson maintained her links with Surrealism by managing the art gallery Guggenheim Jeune from 1938 for the American heiress, Peggy Guggenheim. Henderson expanded his circle of avant-garde acquaintances by helping Marcel Duchamp to hang his show at the gallery. Henderson also showed at Guggenheim Jeune including two of his Surrealist collages in 1938 along with collages by Ernst,

11] Nigel Henderson, photograph taken in Bethnal Green Road in the East End of London during 1950–51

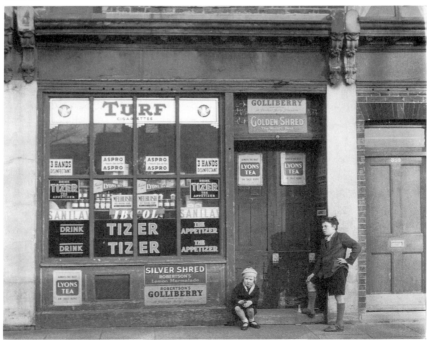

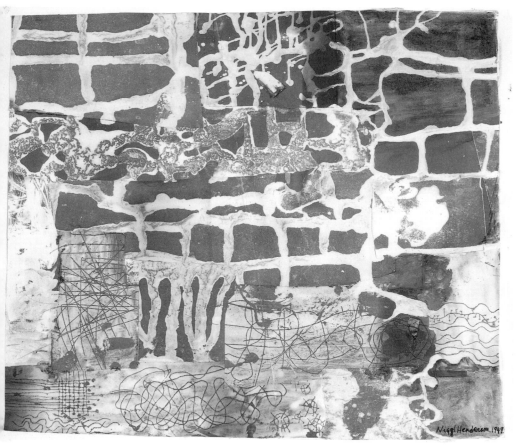

12] Nigel Henderson, *Collage* (1949). Oil and photographic collage mounted on card; purchased from artist by Tate Gallery, 1974

Braque, Picasso, Schwitters and Gris – partly borrowed from Roland Penrose's collection. With the outbreak of war Henderson became a pilot in Coastal Command, resulting in a nervous breakdown after three years of service, at which time he was given less taxing duties. In 1943 Henderson married Judith Stephen, an anthropologist and niece of Vanessa Bell and Virginia Woolf. Judith had recently graduated from Cambridge and introduced Henderson to working-class culture when she was stationed in Bethnal Green London as part of a project run by sociologist, J. L. Petersen. Here, between 1948 and 1952, Henderson photographed his neighbours and surrounding shops with a Schwitters sense of delight in the ordinary (1950–51, Figure 11). The tawdry images of shop frontages and cafés are drily observed with Henderson's ponderous Rolliflex. Henderson also began experimenting with the techniques of photography, enlarging and developing. One result of such technical experiment was *Collage* (1949, Figure 12) in which enlarged fragments of prints were built up into an abstract whole and inscribed with child like scrawls.

Henderson embarked on his career as a fine artist by securing an ex-serviceman's grant to study at the Slade. It was here that Henderson met Eduardo Luigi Paolozzi. Great emphasis has been placed upon Paolozzi's working-class origins in existing accounts of his work, for example:

For this toughie from Leith matured as a sculptor at precisely the moment when those genteel, middle class ideas about art which had operated in Britain for so long most urgently needed a knee in the groin and a butt in the head if British art were ever to become serious.[3]

Another important facet of Paolozzi's image in art history and art criticism is that of the working-class maverick, imbued with the culture of America during his childhood, determined to galvanise the art world with such shocking subject matter in this work. However, whilst Paolozzi did hail from an unusual background, it was certainly not typically working-class in many respects. His parents were Italian immigrants who established an ice-cream business in Edinburgh, and Paolozzi spoke Italian at home. After internment as enemy aliens during the war, Paolozzi left his family to join the Pioneer Corps and in 1944 enrolled as a student at the Slade – then based at the Ashmolean Museum, Oxford. The third future member of the Independent Group to join Paolozzi and Henderson in their admiration for modernism was the sculptor and film-maker, William Turnbull. Having left school at fifteen, Turnbull continued his art education at evening classes and was employed as an illustrator for D. C. Thompson. From 1941 to 1946 Turnbull served as an RAF pilot, which secured his ex-serviceman's grant to study at the Slade full-time. Turnbull shared a broader cultural outlook with Paolozzi and Henderson. The Group rejected Neo-Romanticism, the dominant trend in British art of that time but they did not reject art altogether. Their common interest in popular culture at this time is stressed in existing accounts. However what cemented their friendship and what inspired their work during the late 1940s was their informed enthusiasm for new trends in European modernism, particularly the work of Giacometti and the existentialist philosophy of Jean-Paul Sartre which was such a great influence on the Parisian avant-garde at the time.

Paolozzi confirmed this interest by travelling to Paris in 1947, where he stayed for two years, frequently visited by Turnbull, Henderson and the young art critic, David Sylvester. Paolozzi's trip was financed by the sum of seventy-five pounds, earned through sales at his solo show at the Mayor Gallery, London in January–February 1947. The director of the gallery, F. H. (Freddy) Mayor, was an old acquaintance of Wyn Henderson, and it was through this contact that Paolozzi came to exhibit in London for the first time. As a result of this exhibition Peter Gregory bought *Fisherman and Wife* (1946, Figure 7) for inclusion in the *Forty Years of Modern Art* exhibition. This brightly coloured and roughly executed work was directly inspired by the work of Picasso. Whilst the myth of the Independent Group stresses the importance of contacts made by Paolozzi with ex-GIs and American mass culture in Paris, this was not the main reason for his two-year stay there. Again, the contacts made by Nigel Henderson before the war proved invaluable. Henderson made several trips to Paris during 1947 to 1949, in which he and Paolozzi:

Visited the studios of Brancusi, who lifted and dropped the felt covers of his sculptures with a sort of boat-hook, and Leger, who was encouraging, invited Henderson to his school and showed his film *Ballet Méchanique*. They met Giacometti, Braque and, through Peggy Guggenheim, Arp.[4]

Paolozzi was joined by William Turnbull in the autumn of 1948 and together they visited Musée de l'Homme and the Foyer de l'art brut. Art Brut provided an important source of inspiration for both artists. Indeed, Paolozzi's work was considered close enough to that of Dubuffet to be included in Michel Tapie's *Un Art Autre* (1952). The book incorporated quotes from André Malraux, examples of work by Dubuffet, Alexander Calder, Matta and Jackson Pollock. The Paolozzi work to be included was a sculpture entitled *Concrete* (1951) a roughly inscribed, concrete effigy of an aboriginal head, from the collection of Peter Gregory. Paolozzi's work of the late 1940s was always deliberately crude and rough, drawing from organic and metamorphic references. His third show at the Mayor Gallery in May 1949 comprised drawings and bas-reliefs inspired by images of insects and marine life. Before he left Paris in 1949 Paolozzi completed *Forms on a Bow* (1949, Figure 13) in plaster, exhibited at the Galéries Maeght in the *Les Mains Eblouies* show in October. This was the most successful work to be created by Paolozzi in Paris, and certainly echoes many of the preoccupations of Surrealism, particularly the sadistic spearing of the flaccid forms strung along the bow. Paolozzi returned to London in the autumn of 1949 with his future wife Freda and began teaching textile design part-time at the Central School of Arts and Crafts.

Richard Hamilton shared with Paolozzi and Turnbull the same

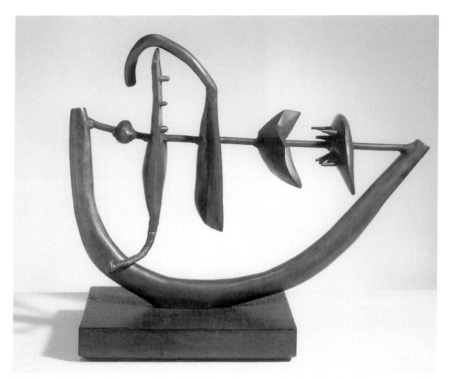

13] Eduardo Paolozzi, *Forms on a Bow* (1949). Cast brass, commissioned by the Contemporary Art Society when the plaster version was shown at the ICA in 1950/51. Presented by the Contemporary Art Society to the Tate Gallery in 1958

original ambition to be a commercial artist. He attended evening classes at St Martin's School of Art until 1938, when he began full-time study at the Royal Academy Schools until their closure in 1940. Hamilton was trained as an engineering draughtsman and in 1941 began work as a jig and tool draughtsman for the Design Unit. In 1942 until 1945 he did the same job for EMI where he worked in the research department. Hamilton returned to his studies at the Royal Academy Schools when they reopened in 1946. However, Hamilton failed to profit from traditional methods of art teaching at the Royal Academy Schools and was expelled. Following eighteen months of military service Hamilton briefly attended a class run by *Vogue* to train fashion illustrators. Hamilton then re-entered fine art education later in 1948, taking up a place at the Slade where he met Nigel Henderson. Through Henderson he acquired a fuller knowledge of modernism. Henderson introduced Hamilton to D'Arcy Wentworth Thompson's *Growth and Form* (1917), Duchamp's *Green Box* and to the epicentre of modernism in Britain, the ICA.

## The ICA headquarters

With the acquisition of 17 Dover Street, Piccadilly in May 1950, the ICA was able to expand its programme considerably and attract a range of new, younger members with the congenial members' room and bar. Previously lectures, readings, film screenings, concerts and discussions had taken place at several obscure venues, including the School of Hygiene and Tropical Medicine and the Egyptian Education Bureau. The ICA's first exhibition at Dover Street was *James Joyce: His Life and Work* which was opened by modernist poet, T. S. Eliot (Figure 14). The help of Richard Hamilton and Nigel Henderson was enlisted and the latter was awarded a one-year honorary membership for lending his mother's copy of *Ulysses* and designing and printing three posters. Richard Hamilton designed the exhibition catalogue in the form of a fold-out, AO sheet in Bauhaus style, particularly inspired by Kurt Schwitters. The Dover Street gallery, clubroom and offices were refurbished during 1950 under the direction of modernist architect, Jane Drew assisted by Neil Morris and Eduardo Paolozzi. Paolozzi decorated the bar area and designed a concrete and metal table with student Terence Conran (Figure 15).

14] Installation shot of the *James Joyce, His Life and Work* exhibition, held at the ICA in 1950. Note Richard Hamilton's poster hanging from the front of the table

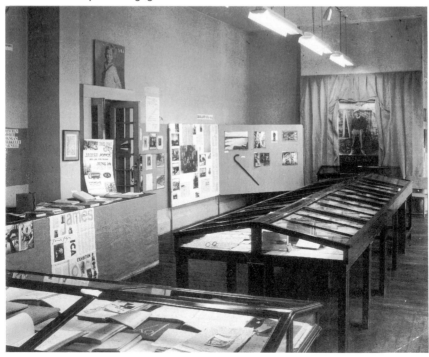

The official opening exhibition of the Dover Street premises was *1950: Aspects of British Art* in December 1950 (Figure 10). Three members of the Independent Group contributed to the show: Paolozzi showed *Forms on a Bow* in plaster. A bronze cast was purchased by the Fine Art Society as a direct result of the exhibition. Turnbull showed *Torque Upwards* (1949, Figure 16) and Hamilton *Microcosmos (Plant Life)* (1950) – an abstract work based on *Growth and Form*. Reviews of the show reveal the general unpopularity of modern art at this time: beyond the tight circles of the ICA, no distinction was made between Abstraction and Surrealism; it was simply all modern art. The *Guardian* critic was offended by the 'oppressive cleverness' of some exhibits, whilst James Dudley complained that it 'shows the complete bankruptcy and poverty of thoughts and ideas about life current in certain sections of the art world.'[5] Therefore, whilst such critics as Dudley and John Berger were supporting the case for realism, and the Arts Council was advocating a patriotic Neo-Romanticism, the ICA publicised the case for

15] Eduardo Paolozzi and Terence Conran, table design for ICA's new Dover Street premises in challenging concrete and metal

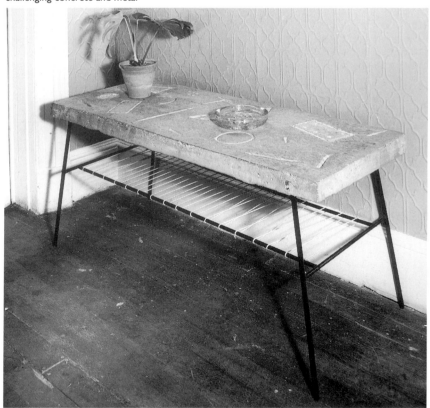

international, experimental art – very often with a Surrealist bias.

During the Festival year of 1951 most galleries and institutions contributed towards the celebration of national culture. The ICA proved to be the exception by exhibiting the work of Roberto Matta and Picasso and screening French Surrealist films. During 1951 Paolozzi's links with the ICA were strengthened; he was made an honorary member in April and Freda Elliot, whom he married in 1951, began working at the ICA as a gallery assistant. Paolozzi again exhibited in an ICA show of young artists held at the Warner Theatre in Leicester Square.[6] Paolozzi was also responsible for decorating the gallery of Dover Street for the 1951 New Year's Eve party, together with another future Independent Group member, Toni del Renzio.

Toni del Renzio was to provide the Independent Group with an important link back to war-time Surrealism in London. He had been a member of E. L. T. Mesens's Surrealist group, only to form a splinter group after his marriage to the Surrealist painter, Ithel

16] William Turnbull, *Torque Upwards* (1949) as shown at *1950 Aspects of British Art*

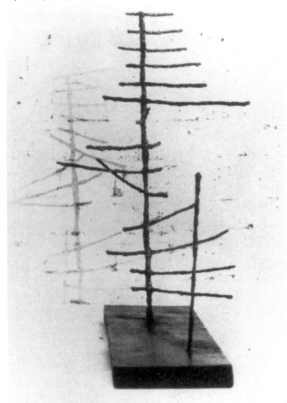

Colquhoun. This resulted in the publication of a Surrealist pamphlet entitled *Arson* in March 1942 and the editing, by del Renzio, of a Surrealist section of *New Road 1943* at the invitation of Alex Comfort and John Bayliss. However, the Mesens group continued to represent British Surrealism officially, culminating in the 'Déclaration du groupe surréaliste en Angleterre' in *Le Surréalisme en 1947*, published in Paris in connection with an International Surrealist exhibition at Galéries Maeght. The declaration was signed by four founding members of the ICA: Penrose, Brunius, Mesens and Melville.

## Growth and Form

As the ICA matured through 1951 with an expanded programme, facilitated by new premises, so future members of the Independent Group became increasingly active at the Institute. The exhibition *Growth and Form* (Figures 17 and 18) represents the first major involvement of Richard Hamilton at the ICA and illuminates the complex relationship which existed between the ICA's founders and the younger members of the future Independent Group. *Growth and Form* (1917) by D'Arcy Wentworth Thompson was current reading among British artists in post-war Britain, particularly the Constructivists. Nigel Henderson and Richard Hamilton agreed that it could form the basis of an exciting exhibition. Through Henderson's pre-war contacts he was able to approach Roland Penrose and suggest that the exhibition be held at the ICA. Penrose first drew the attention of his fellow committee members to the exhibition proposal on 13 April 1949, suggesting that the Institute should sponsor *Growth and Form* as part of the Festival of Britain. Herbert Read opposed Penrose's proposal on the grounds that it did not conform with the Festival's theme – one hundred years of British achievement. Read was more informed of the plans for the Festival of Britain, as he had been a member of the Arts Council's Art Panel since the retirement of Leigh Ashton and Duncan Grant in 1947. Such divisions were continually apparent on the Managing Committee and such schisms were to be reflected in the relationship with the Independent Group. From the first meeting of the Group early in 1952 to its demise three years later, a symbiotic relationship with the ICA existed and cross-overs between the two were both multifarious and reciprocal.

The future of the *Growth and Form* exhibition, for instance, was ensured when Penrose suggested the formation of a planning committee specifically for it. Although the exhibition fell within the

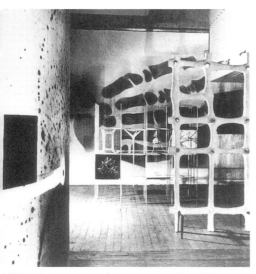

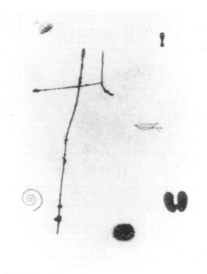

17] Installation shot of *Growth and Form*, ICA, 1951

18] Richard Hamilton, *Heteromorphism* (1951). Hard and soft-ground etching, drypoint and aquatint. Used as the front cover for the *Growth and Form* catalogue

general aims of the ICA, the Managing Committee was dubious about allowing a young student to be exclusively responsible for its organisation, under the auspices of the ICA. The newly formed committee first met on 31 January 1950 under the chairmanship of J. R. M. Brumwell. Initially the ICA was not in a position to offer financial assistance or a venue for the project. Although the ICA was soon to take over the Dover Street premises, this was thought to be unsuitable, as Hamilton's ambition was to mount the exhibition in a large hall. However, Hamilton and the *Growth and Form* sub-committee failed to attract any sponsorship by September 1950, and so the exhibition was scaled down for Dover Street.

Although no financial backing was secured from industry, with the exception of £50 from Metal Box Co. Ltd, several sympathetic companies donated services or materials. Metal Box and Carlton Artists undertook much of the photographic work, vital for the success of the exhibition, and Rank loaned film projectors. This experimental show was divided into seventeen categories, each illustrating a separate aspect of the structure of growth and natural forms, ranging from atomic particles to astronomy. Hamilton created a complete environment with the exhibition – blown up microphotographs and X-rays were incorporated on to screens, films showing crystal growth and the maturation of a sea urchin were projected on to the walls in order that the spectator be totally engulfed. The exhibition only attracted 1,140 visitors and lost £223, a sum which was underwritten by the ICA.

The crucial link between Thompson's thesis and the Independent Group was the rejection of teleological, universal explanations of the environment. In the introduction to *Growth and Form* Thompson criticised Charles Darwin, among others, because 'it has been by way of the final cause, by the teleological concept of end . . . that men have been chiefly wont to explain the living world.'[7] Thompson understood that physical science should seek to explain the construction, growth and working of living phenomena in terms of the causal relationship between growth and form. Hence, the scientist should deal with the 'ephemeral and accidental, not eternal nor universal things.'[8] Thompson's rejection of Aristotelian philosophy was crucial for the Independent Group's understanding of art, design and mass culture. This view was reinforced by the influential writing of art historian and Director of the Warburg Institute, Ernst Gombrich. In the book published in conjunction with the exhibition, *Aspects of Form* (1951) Gombrich contributed the essay, 'Meditations on a Hobby Horse or the Roots of Artistic Form' in which he criticised 'the age-old problem of universals as applied to art. It has received its classical formulation in the Platonising theories of the Academicians.'[9] Gombrich advocated the use of iconology for the understanding of visual culture, to create a more rigorous and scientific approach which superseded German formal analysis. Using iconology the individual reactions to visual imagery could be more fully understood as could the specifics of individual creativity. What the two authors shared was a dismissal of the Enlightenment concept of universality in favour of an empirical approach. Further ammunition for the attack on traditional aesthetics was exploited by the Independent Group from the work of Siegfried Giedion. In his initial draft proposal for *Growth and Form*, Hamilton had quoted from Giedion in order to clarify his aim:

The most obvious benefits of the exhibition would be the influence it may have upon design trends. The general implications are very wide: S. Giedion in his study of mechanisation says 'The evolution from material and mechanistic conceptions must start from a new insight into the nature of matter and organisms'. The exhibition should also make its contribution in this direction.[10]

Giedion had taken it almost for granted in *Mechanization takes Command* (1948) that the artist of the twentieth century had accepted a non-Aristotelian approach to change. Such artists:

resort to elements such as machines, mechanisms, and ready-made articles as some of the few true products of the period, to liberate themselves from the ruling taste.[11]

In this context, Giedion was discussing the work of Dada and Marcel Duchamp in particular. The Independent Group saw itself as forming part of this lineage, and based its critique of contemporary British aesthetics upon the non-Aristotelian approach of Giedion, Gombrich and Thompson. Lawrence Alloway, who was to convene the 1955 session of the Independent Group, wrote a eulogy to Dada in 1956. He praised its 'acceptance of the multiple value of life' saying that 'it does not insist upon the abstraction of fixed aspects of life for aesthetic treatment. It effectually consigns art to the tangled channels of everyday communications. A work of art may be made of bus tickets or it may look like an advertisement. It may be an ad.'[12]

This flew in the face of the ICA management who did not critically analyse the achievements of modernism. Indeed, the work of Herbert Read acted as a focus for the entire Independent Group in its criticism of the sterility of an unquestioning approach to modernism. Read's basic hypothesis of *The Philosophy of Modern Art* (1951) had been:

There is no phase in art, from the palaeolithic cave paintings to the latest developments in constructivism that does not seem to me to be an illustration of the biological and teleological significance of the aesthetic activity in man.[13]

Read emphasises the timelessness and everlasting qualities of beauty, using Arisotelian philosophy as the basis for his argument. Such aesthetic theories were anathema to the Independent Group, whose approach to 'beauty' was certainly not classical but pragmatic. Richard Hamilton recalled that 'if there was one binding spirit among the people of the Independent Group it was a distaste for Herbert Read's attitudes.'[14] Alloway and the Independent Group strove to rid art criticism of 'these obstinate absolutes'[15] by rejecting Read's metaphysical analysis of visual culture and formulating an Expendable Aesthetic during their meetings from 1952 to 1955.

## The Young/Independent Group

By the end of January 1952, what became known as the Independent Group was beginning to take shape. At the very first meeting of the ICA's sub-committee on visiting lecture policy,

Anthony Kloman the Director of Publicity at the ICA, reported that a group of young members wished to organise lectures for themselves. For convenience sake these members were referred to as the 'Young Group'. Credit for its formation should be given to Dorothy Morland, then Assistant Director of the ICA and marginalised in existing accounts of the Group, possibly because of her gender. The consensus of opinion among Richard Hamilton, Nigel Henderson, Toni del Renzio, Reyner Banham and Richard Lannoy indicates that this circle of young members was dissatisfied with performing menial tasks for the ICA and wanted to make more of an impact on the programme of events. Richard Lannoy, a photographer who was then working as gallery assistant at the ICA, approached Dorothy Morland with a list of names and the suggestion that a nucleus of young members should hold regular discussion sessions. Morland was in agreement and she facilitated the first meetings of the Young Group in early 1952. She continued to support the Group during its lifespan, defending it at Managing Committee level, attending some meetings herself and encouraging members to repeat their talks in more polished form before a wider ICA public. Reyner Banham referred to Morland as their 'Guardian Angel' in the interview he conducted with her for the *Fathers of Pop* film.

The first meeting of the Group consisted of Eduardo Paolozzi feeding a series of coloured images taken from American magazine advertising through an epidiascope. These images have subsequently acquired a mythical aura, often cited as the first examples of British Pop Art or even Pop Art. Later used to form the *Bunk* prints of 1972, the images fall within the established canon of twentieth-century collage and photomontage (Figure 19). The Dada group in particular, whom the Independent Group identified themselves with, used the techniques of manipulating images from mass culture to create startling works of art from 1920 onwards. The work of Hannah Hoch, Raoul Hausmann, Max Ernst and Francis Picabia established the conventions of the medium. Collage was then used by the Surrealists to evoke strange visions, again manipulating found images from mass culture. Indeed, three members of the ICA management, Penrose, Brunius and Mesens had used collage extensively throughout the 1930s and 1940s and it continued to be shown at the ICA during the post-war years. Lawrence Alloway celebrated collage in an exhibition he organised at the ICA during 1954. *Collages and Objects* included pre-war work by Picasso, Ernst, Duchamp, Schwitters and Eluard. Penrose and Mesens were also included as well as the contemporary work of

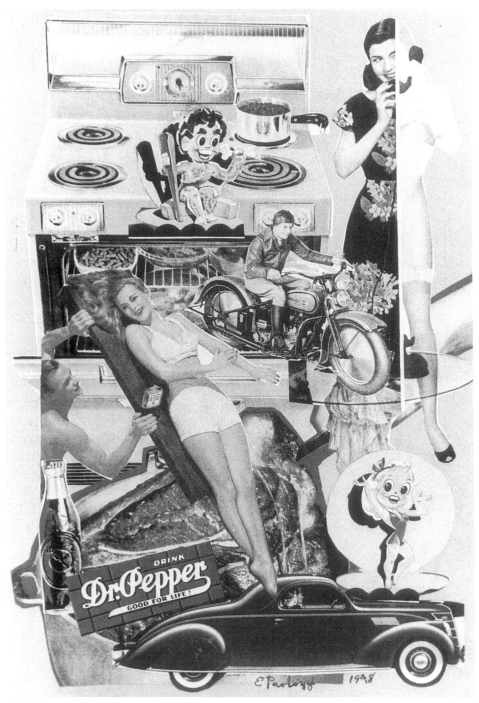

19] Eduardo Paolozzi, *Dr Pepper* (1948). Collage on paper.
A representative sample of the mass media images which the
Independent Group avidly collected

Dubuffet and Independent Group members Paolozzi, McHale and Henderson. This meeting established the framework for future events – a small number of key individuals brought together on a quest to re-evaluate modernism, huddled into a small room in Mayfair.

The second session of the fledgling Independent Group consisted of a talk by Alfred Jules Ayer, the most prominent British exponent of the philosophy of logical positivism. His book, *Language, Truth and Logic* (1936) reworked the thinking of the Vienna Circle, particularly Schlick and Carnap, of the inter-war years into a British context. Although this may seem an extraordinary departure in the light of the Group's interest in visual culture, it can be explained as a reinforcement of the non-Aristotelian standpoint. In his complete rejection of all metaphysical statements as unverifiable by experience, Ayer provided the Group with a valuable philosophical framework for defining its position against that of Herbert Read. During April 1952 there was one more meeting of the Group where they discussed the work of a North American kinetic artist Edward Hoppe.

The Young Group disbanded on Lannoy's departure to India in July 1952. The convenorship officially passed to Toni del Renzio. Through his Surrealist contacts del Renzio had been involved at the ICA since the opening of the *40,000 Years of Modern Art* show. He travelled to Italy during 1951 sponsored by Peter Watson, and his proposal to mount an exhibition of designer furniture at the ICA was accepted. He was then employed as a part-time bar manager at the Institute and was approached to convene the Young Group. However, del Renzio's energies were largely devoted to his *Tomorrow's Furniture* exhibition which opened on 5 June 1952. The show drew on the challenging approach of the Independent Group to modernism, celebrating the work of modernist designers but drawing attention to the achievements of post-war Italian, Scandinavian and American design in the catalogue introduction, written by del Renzio. Del Renzio also made reference to the writing of Giedion and stressed the importance of ongoing technological innovation in design – a theme to be fully explored in the Group's creation of the Expendable Aesthetic. The exhibition consisted of prototype chairs, lighting and shelving by leading British designers including Ernest Race, Clive Latimer and Robin Day with a ceiling canopy designed by Paolozzi. The Group failed to meet formally throughout the summer of 1952 and was to reconvene successfully in the autumn of 1952 under the able leadership of Peter Reyner Banham.

## The Machine Aesthetic

The theme for this first full term of the Independent Group sprang from Banham's own interests at that time. Registered for a further degree, which he completed at the Courtauld Institute of Art London, Banham published his thesis as *Theory and Design in the First Machine Age* in 1960. Although his research was supervised by Nikolaus Pevsner, Banham endeavoured to show, by explaining the emergence of the International Style, that the history of the modern movement could not be fully conveyed by his supervisor's concept of an apostolic succession of design heroes. Banham located the Futurists within the history of modern design, an omission on Pevsner's part. Banham was to explain the significance of the Futurists for the Independent Group in a programme entitled 'Primitives of a Mechanised Art' which he made as part of the BBC's *Art-Anti-Art* series in 1959. Drawing direct parallels between the Futurists and the Independent Group, Banham argued that fine art could no longer function in its traditional form, and must acknowledge the impact of mechanisation. Banham's conclusion to the programme rewrites a Futurist manifesto for the Independent Group:

Boccioni in *Pittura Scultura Futurista* demands the abolition of art, and replaces the vacuum with 'café-chantant, gramophone, cinema, electric advertising, mechanistic architecture, skyscrapers . . . nightlife . . . speed, automobiles, aeroplanes'. Alter café-chantant just enough to mean Espresso Bar (or even popular music, which Boccioni praised elsewhere) the rest follows naturally – hi-fi, cinemascope, the lights in Piccadilly Circus, curtain-walled office blocks – indeed, the last four terms, night-life, speed, automobiles, aeroplanes, don't need altering at all. These images describe the London scene into which we stepped as we left the ICA those evenings in 1953 and 1954 . . . No wonder we found in them long-lost ancestors of our own pre-occupations, right down to the details.[16]

It was science, technology and the history of design which formed the focus of the Independent Group meetings from September 1952 to June 1953. When Banham took up the convenorship Dorothy Morland referred to it as 'our Young Independent Group'.[17] The 'Young' was eventually dropped and the title of 'Independent Group' was first used in an ICA Managing Committee meeting on 12 November 1952, when, upon reading a report from Banham, it was agreed that the Group should be encouraged. Although difficult to reconcile with the environmental concerns of the late-twentieth century, the Group shared an uncritical appreciation of new technology with the rest of western society. In *Theory and Design in the First Machine Age* Banham described the

1950s as the 'Jet Age, the Detergent Decade, the Second Industrial Revolution'.[18] This evolutionary view of scientific discovery evolving towards greater and greater improvements was drawn from mass culture and conflicted with the notion of universal beauty advocated by the ICA management and Herbert Read in particular. Unlike their elders at the ICA, the Independent Group had extensive experience of working directly with technology and the products of scientific research. Banham had worked in the aircraft industry before he began his art history training, Hamilton had worked as an engineering draughtsman; Sam Stevens, James Stirling and Sandy Wilson would be familiar with technological discoveries through their architectural backgrounds and Nigel Henderson and William Turnbull through their flying experience during the war. The Independent Group sought to broaden their knowledge of science and technology by inviting various experts to address their meetings.

One such lecture was delivered to the Independent Group by the De Havilland helicopter designer, J. S. Shapiro, and was entitled 'The Helicopter as an Example of Technical Development'. Norman Pirie, a microbiologist, talked to the Group on the subject of 'Are Proteins Unique?', an area of interest which linked back to the *Growth and Form* exhibition. The philosophical questions thrown up by the show were further explored in a discussion entitled 'Were the Dadaists Non-Aristotelian?'. According to Frank Whitford, Banham contributed a lecture to this early programme on the Machine Aesthetic.[19] This seems likely, as Toni del Renzio had indicated to the Exhibitions Sub-Committee that Banham was 'anxious to give a lecture, the Machine Aesthetic in the Modern Movement'[20] suggesting that Banham had already delivered such a lecture to the Independent Group. As was often to be the case with the Group's programme, talks were often repeated in a more finished form before a wider audience of ICA members. However, Banham's lecture never formed part of the ICA's programme, but this particular formulation of a critique of modernism was published by *Architectural Review* in April 1955. 'Machine Aesthetic' and a lengthy article, 'Industrial Design and Popular Art' published in the Italian design journal, *Civiltà delle Macchine* in November of the same year, act as a convenient summary of the achievements of the first session of the Independent Group. In both pieces Banham stressed that the architects of the modern movement lacked an understanding of engineering. They utilised their superficial and misguided concept of the engineer as 'noble savage' to advocate their own aesthetic prejudices. Architects, most notably Le

Corbusier, maintained that the engineer was working with reference only to pure function, and that this automatically produced geometrical form. Banham argued that this was acceptable during the 1920s as car and aeroplane design were at an early stage of development and indeed were geometrical and corresponded visually to the forms of modern architecture. From this observation the modern movement architects argued that the style they designed in was wholly utilitarian and objective, without aesthetic bias.

Banham countered this claim to objectivity by arguing that product design of the 1950s did not measure up to the functionalist criteria. From his experience in the aircraft industry Banham knew that technology was never static and new techniques and materials were perpetually being incorporated into design. Banham also argued that functional concerns were not the sole determinants of design; there were other design factors to be considered such as social prestige, costing, ornamentation and styling innovations. Thus modernism was no more than an architectural style, the roots of which lay in classicism. It is indicative of the Independent Group's ambivalent attitude to modern architecture that they contributed extensively to an exhibition of Le Corbusier's work. A selection of his paintings, drawings, sculptures and tapestries was shown at the ICA in April and May 1953. Colin St John Wilson wrote the catalogue introduction and the catalogue itself was designed by Toni del Renzio. During May 1953 Banham contributed towards a *Points of View* discussion on the exhibition with Wells Coates, Victor Pasmore, Leslie Martin and Wilson. The Independent Group presented an evening's session with colour slides on *The Work of Le Corbusier* during the same month.

The controversial nature of the Independent Group's activities is illustrated by Herbert Read's rebuffal of Morland's suggestion that the Group should meet with Le Corbusier when he visited the exhibition. Instead, members of the Independent Group were to fulfil their usual role of helping with the mounting of exhibitions with, for example, Richard Hamilton designing the catalogue for the Max Ernst exhibition in 1952 as well as contributing to the *Young Painters* show of the same year and designing the layout with his wife, Terry Hamilton, for the *Wonder and Horror of the Human Head* exhibition of 1953 (Figure 20).

By May 1953 the Independent Group had carved an identity for itself at the ICA as a focus for research and innovative, if unpalatable, ideas on modernism. The separate strands which fed into this development had been British philosophy, the history of technology and design, mass culture and a re-evaluation of modern archi-

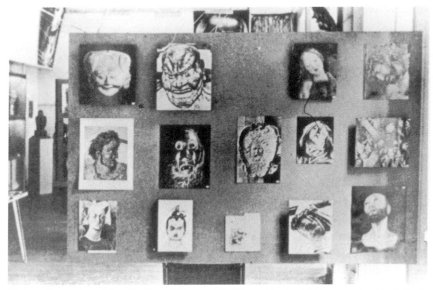

**20]** Installation shot of the *Wonder and Horror of the Human Head* exhibition organised by Roland Penrose in 1953

tecture. From this point the Group developed two public manifestations of its research – the exhibition, *Parallel of Life and Art* and a lecture programme, *Aesthetic Problems of Contemporary Art* (Appendix 1).

## Notes

1 For a fuller analysis of the historiography of the Independent Group see A. Massey and P. Sparke, 'The Myth of the Independent Group', *Block* No. 10, 1985.

2 See Hugh Ford, Foreword to *These Were the Hours: Memoirs of My Hours Press, Reanville and Paris 1928–31*. Feffer & Simons, London, 1968, p. xiv.

3 *Eduardo Paolozzi*, Arts Council exhibition catalogue, 1976, p. 7.

4 *Nigel Henderson*, exhibition catalogue, Anthony d'Offay, 1977, p. 7.

5 'The Clever and the Violent', *Manchester Guardian*, 15 December 1950. J. Dudley, 'Artists in a Morass', *Daily Worker*, 27 December 1950.

6 Paolozzi showed *Study for Cage* (1951, plaster on wire) the maquette for his Festival of Britain contribution, exhibited at the RBA Galleries with the *60 for '51* show. Paolozzi also showed *Forms on a Bow* (1951, welded steel); William Turnbull showed *Caged Bird* (undated, copper) and Richard Hamilton showed two abstract canvases, *Microcosmos (Chromatic Spiral)* and *Microcosmos (Induction)* both of 1950.

7 D. W. Thompson, *Growth and Form*, London, 1917, p. 6.

8 *Ibid.* p. 6.

9 E. H. Gombrich, 'Meditations on a Hobby Horse or the Roots of Artistic Form' in Lancelot Law Whyte (ed.) *Aspects of Form* (first published 1951), Lund Humphries, 1968, p. 210.

10  Draft proposal for *Growth and Form* 1949, p. 1, ICA Archives.

11  S. Giedion, *Mechanization Takes Command*, New York, 1948, p. 44.

12  L. Alloway, 'Dada 1956', *Architectural Design*, November 1956, p. 374.

13  H. Read, *The Philosophy of Modern Art*, Faber & Faber, 1951, p. 13.

14  R. Hamilton, in *Fathers of Pop* in discussion with Richard Hamilton, Reyner Banham and Lawrence Alloway, 25 May 1977, p. 4.

15  L. Alloway, *Nine Abstract Artists*, Alec Tiranti, 1954, p. 1.

16  R. Banham, 'Primitives of a Mechanised Art', broadcast as part of the BBC's *Art-Anti-Art*, 21 November 1959. *Art-Anti-Art* was a series of fifteen programmes on the Third Programme, produced by Leonie Cohn, a member of the ICA Managing Committee from October 1954. Possibly through this connection the Independent Group contributed to three of the programmes during 1959 and 1960. On 13 November 1959 Richard Hamilton discussed a taped interview with Marcel Duchamp, his great hero. The series ended on 11 March 1960 with a discussion between Lawrence Alloway, Eduardo Paolozzi, Richard Hamilton and Basil Taylor entitled *Artists as Consumers, the Splendid Bargain*, in which the artist's position vis-à-vis American popular culture was explored.

17  Unpublished letter from Dorothy Morland to Christian Simpson, 29 September 1952, ICA Archives. Simpson, a BBC producer, lectured at the ICA on 23 September 1952 on 'Movement for the Screen'. In her letter of thanks, Morland mentioned the Group: 'It was very good of you to say you would come along sometime and talk to our Young Independent Group.'

18  R. Banham, *Theory and Design in the First Machine Age*, Architectural Press, 1960, p. 9.

19  F. Whitford, *Paolozzi*, Tate Gallery Exhibition Catalogue, 1971, p. 44.

20  ICA, Exhibitions Sub-Committee, 11 March 1953, ICA Archives.

# 4

# Aesthetic Problems of Contemporary Art

THE TITLE of a course of nine seminars which the Independent Group ran from October 1953 until February 1954 was *Aesthetic Problems of Contemporary Art* (see Appendix 1). The course offered a revisionist perspective on modernism, informed by the discussions around new technology which was a key feature of the first session of the Independent Group. For the Group, visual culture did not exist in a vacuum, as the ICA management purists supposed, but in direct relation to science and technology. It was this belief which also inspired the exhibition, *Parallel of Life and Art*, held at the ICA during September and October 1953 and organised by Paolozzi, Henderson and Alison and Peter Smithson. The Group extended the perimeters of aesthetic debate by acknowledging scientific developments in discussions about art.

*Aesthetic Problems of Contemporary Art* marked a new phase in the relationship between the Independent Group and the ICA management. Previously the Group had met informally and privately whilst performing menial tasks at the Dover Street premises. With the appointment of Herbert Read to the Charles Eliot Norton Chair of Poetry at Harvard and his departure to America in September 1953 for a seven-month lecture tour, a replacement was needed on the Managing Committee. The Independent Group's advocate, Dorothy Morland, suggested that:

the Independent Group should be asked to make one or two suggestions for consideration by the Managing Committee. She said they were a lively and intelligent body of young people, and she felt they would be encouraged if they could be given a measure of responsibility for the ICA's activities.[1]

Reyner Banham was duly nominated by the Independent Group and co-opted by the Managing Committee on 24 June 1953. At the same meeting Dorothy Morland proposed that the Independent Group should run a lecture series on 'Problems of Aesthetics' with critic Robert Melville in the chair and Reyner Banham acting as convenor. The Managing Committee, which consisted of the 1946 stalwarts Roland Penrose, Peter Gregory and Peter Watson together with Stephen Spender, were reticent in their acceptance of the proposal. Doubting the ability of this querulous, inexperienced but ambitious collection of young men to run such a course to the standards of the ICA, they stipulated that: 'the series was announced as sponsored by the Independent Group.'[2] The programme eventually ran from 15 October 1953 to 25 February 1954 within the auspices of the ICA, probably after lobbying from Morland to overturn the initial ruling of the Managing Committee.

The ICA had run events in the past on the relationship between art and science. For example in 1953 Professor J. Z. Young of the Anatomy Department, University College London, talked about 'The Creative Activities of the Human Brain' followed by a discussion chaired by A. J. Ayer. However, there was never any serious attempt to discuss art and science in conjunction with each other and the concept that new discoveries in science could determine style in art and design was never considered. *Aesthetic Problems of Contemporary Art* challenged the mainstream, ICA view of the relationship between art, design and science. For the ICA management, exciting breakthroughs were made in painting by the individual genius and then explained by science – painting and sculpture always topped that triangular framework within which they categorised cultural production. The Independent Group was proposing a linear framework, without hierarchies, with which to analyse art and science. The main objective of the course was to identify the problems facing contemporary painters, sculptors, designers and architects. The source of such contemporary problems was seen as emanating from new, scientific discoveries. The impetus for the course was a series of four illustrated lectures given by Herbert Read earlier in 1953. Entitled *The Aesthetics of Sculpture*, Read's discussion focused on the problems of handling space, mass, movement and figuration in order to create a dynamism in static sculpture. This built on the ideas he had expressed in 1951 in *Contemporary British Art*:

Vitality in organic objects is an effect of movement – either the immediate movements of muscles, or the slow movement of growth. The sculptor's problem is to give this dynamic quality to objects which do not move or grow. It is done by establishing certain relations between a solid mass and its surrounding space.[3]

William Turnbull and Fello Atkinson contradicted this approach in their session, 'New Concepts of Space' where they argued that solid mass had been superseded by 'ideas of penetrability and transparency.'[4] *Aesthetic Problems of Contemporary Art* also heralded the first involvement of Lawrence Alloway in Independent Group events. Alloway was working as a visiting lecturer at the Tate Gallery and at the Courtauld Institute of Art. He had also contributed to mainstream ICA events since 1952, with a *Points of View* discussion on recent sculpture shows. He continued to speak at the *Points of View* sessions during early 1953 and also gave two lectures – 'The Human Head in Modern Art' in conjunction with *The Wonder and Horror of the Human Head* show and 'British Painting in the Fifties'. By this time, Alloway was a great admirer of the work of both Paolozzi and Turnbull and lavished praise on their work in his first piece for *Art News* in the summer of 1953.[5] For *The Aesthetic Problems of Contemporary Art* Alloway had the gall to give his seminar the same title as one of Read's lectures, except that he discussed mass culture within the criterion of 'The Human Image' which Read most certainly did not. The course leaflet also emphasised that the general problems confronting the entire range of the visual arts were being addressed and not the narrow consideration of one area, as Read's series had done.

Banham opened the series with a discussion of the notion proposed by Siegfried Giedion, that new technology had made a tremendous impact not only on industrial design, but also on the fine arts. Banham spoke of 'the status of the work of art itself, through the growth of techniques of mass production.'[6] Richard Hamilton discussed the challenges created by the impact of technology, from microphotography to astronomy, on source material for the artist, thus extending the concerns of *Growth and Form*. Sandy Wilson dealt with the problems facing the architect and artist by new research in the area of natural symmetry. Toni del Renzio's lecture, 'Non-Formal Painting', explored new concepts of space and American Abstract Expressionism. The impetus for the paper came from the *Opposing Forces* exhibition, held at the ICA during January 1953, which included work by Jackson Pollock, Sam Francis and Georges Methieu. This first London showing of what was to be the most important movement in painting in the 1950s certainly impressed the Independent Group. Robert Melville also referred to contemporary developments in American painting with his reference to Jungian psychoanalysis and the concept of myth in his session, 'Mythology and Psychology'. For Alloway, Jackson Pollock was certainly the most important and exciting contemporary painter to be seen in London: 'not so much as a painter, but for his images . . . because the drip paintings appeared to be examples of disorder and yet contained as works of art. I think that meant quite a lot to Eduardo and ideologically to a lot of us'.[7] The work of Jackson Pollock was also to be featured in the second manifestation of the Independent Group at the ICA in 1953, the exhibition *Parallel of Life and Art* (Figure 21).

A coterie of young architects and artists had formed at the Central School of Arts and Crafts, London: Eduardo Paolozzi, Victor Pasmore and Peter Smithson were all teaching there during 1952 and first proposed the idea of a group exhibition to the ICA Managing Committee in March 1952 via Dorothy Morland. The Group was asked to re-submit in six months' time and the idea was finally agreed in January 1953 with the support of Roland Penrose and financial guarantees from Peter Gregory, Roland Jenkins (the Smithsons' engineer and Ove Arup's partner), Jane Drew and Denys Lasdun. The architect Peter Smithson had designed Hunstanton School, the antithesis of the New Empiricism, in 1949 with his wife Alison. It was Paolozzi who then introduced the Smithsons to Nigel Henderson at his home in Bethnal Green during 1952. The four discovered that they shared a common enthusiasm for visual imagery which was not usually regarded as being of significance artistically. This informal group, an offshoot of the Independent Group, then continued to meet and pool resources. Discussions centred on images found in newspapers, magazines and scientific books which were then selected to form the exhibition, *Parallel of Life and Art*. Although the images derived from a vast array of sources, their apparent incongruity was overcome by presenting all the images as photographs, printed on coarse, grainy paper and mounted on cardboard. The exhibition was staged as a total environment, like *Growth and Form*, with images hung from the ceiling and obscuring the walls.

This was a polemical exhibition: it challenged the viewer's perception of what was beautiful and worthy of inclusion in an art gallery. The exhibits were drawn largely from scientific and technical sources, including diagrams and photographs of radio valves, televisions and spacesuits. There were also images which derived from the application of technology to the reproduction of visual material, such as radiographs and microphotographs. The remainder of the images could be loosely described as anthropological, and included scenes from tribal ceremonies and non-western dwellings.

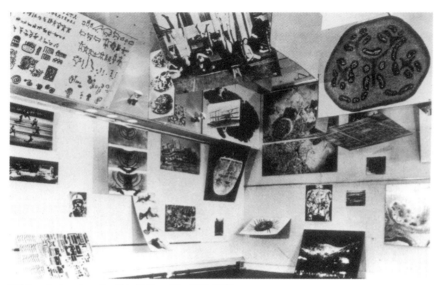

21] Installation shot, *Parallel of Life and Art*, ICA, 1953

22] Front cover of the *Parallel of Life and Art* exhibition catalogue based upon an X-ray image of a man shaving, illustrated in Moholy-Nagy's *Vision in Motion* (1947)

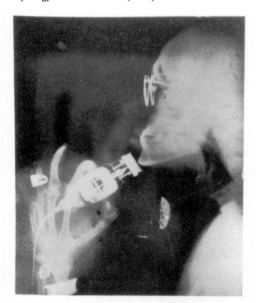

CATALOGUE OF THE EXHIBITION

## Parallel of Life and Art

*Held at the Institute of Contemporary Arts*

*September 11th to October 18th, 1953.*

The continuity of the exhibition was extended even to works of art by the use of photography (Figure 22). The work of Jackson Pollock was not included but there was a photograph of him working in his studio from a famous series, published in *Life* magazine by Hans Namuth. As Alloway recalled:

These photographs of Hans Namuth showing Jackson Pollock at work were quite well known in England because they were reproduced earlier in a portfolio, a whole bunch of them . . . and Toni del Renzio had a copy of the portfolio and we all saw the thing.[8]

Original works by Henderson and Paolozzi were not exhibited in their own right but as photographs. For example, *Plaster Blocks* (1952) by Paolozzi was incorporated as a photograph by Henderson, and a photo-image of coffee grounds by Henderson was included in the Landscape section. Henderson was currently experimenting with the manipulation of the photographic process by spreading used coffee on the light-sensitive paper to produce an image with coarse texture.

The exhibits shared overall a certain crudeness, vulgarity and rawness. The microphotographs were not of pretty snowflakes but of benign tumours and rats. The technical photographs were of missiles, insects and vegetable tissue. The photographs taken from newspapers, such as the funeral of King George VI and a burnt-out forest, represented gloomy events. It was this disregard for conventional aesthetics which located the exhibition within the Anti-Art and Art Brut traditions and offended many visitors. The show was visited by 443 members over the five weeks of its opening and provided the basis for Banham's formulation of the concept of New Brutalism, which he outlined in an article of the same name in *Architectural Review*, December 1955.

Following the showing of *Parallel of Life and Art* at the ICA at Dover Street, the panels were moved to the Architectural Association in Bedford Square, London, where a stormy discussion took place on 2 December 1953 led by the show's organisers. Reyner Banham referred to the debate in his article 'New Brutalism' which celebrated the work of the Smithsons:

students at the Architectural Association complained of the deliberate flouting of the traditional concepts of photographic beauty, of the cult of ugliness and 'denying the spiritual in Man'[7]

The images which made up *Parallel of Life and Art* were deliberately not pleasing to the eye. Paolozzi, Henderson and the Smithsons were presenting the visual equivalent to the *Aesthetic Problems of Contemporary Art* seminar course, in exploring the impact of technology on the visual arts and on the practising artist or architect. Bryan Robertson of the Whitechapel Art Gallery, recorded this aspect of the show in *Art News and Review*: 'the exhibition also leaves the spectator with the feeling that the barriers between the artist, the scientist and the technician are dissolving in a singularly potent way.'[8] The Independent Group aimed to break down these barriers in its meetings, seminar course and in *Parallel of Life and Art*. The Group succeeded in dissolving traditional divisions between science and art through the creation of a new aesthetic critique. Banham explained this new understanding within Anti-Art terms, using the concept of 'image':

Ultimately . . . it means something which is virtually valuable, but not necessarily by the standards of classical aesthetics . . . for the New Brutalists' interests in image are commonly regarded, by many of themselves as well as their critics, as being anti-art, or at any rate, anti-beauty in the classical aesthetic sense of the word.[9]

The Independent Group saw the need for a new aesthetic understanding, as the art of the post-war era could not be fully understood using the outdated tools of Aristotelian philosophy as proposed by Herbert Read. It did not judge a painting by how well it measured up to an abstract and absolute notion such as beauty. Toni del Renzio made reference to this in his discussion of abstract painting on the seminar course. 'Non-Formal Painting' defined works of art concerned with Aristotelian ideals as 'formal'. The discussion was concerned with a 'crisis of signification, shifting the value of the work of art from the thing signified to the act of signification itself, bringing to a head certain latent tendencies of abstract art hitherto held in check by formal preoccupations.'[10] The work was self-referential, turned in on itself by a new technological sensibility. This redefinition of the meaning which a work of art could encapsulate was central to the Group's overall understanding of all cultural artefacts. If the painting, the scientific diagram, the film or the American car contained its own discrete system of signification, then no hierarchy could exist between 'high' and 'low' culture and the established, modern canon of taste could not operate. This new aesthetic perspective was informed largely by cultural criticism being formulated across the Atlantic and it was Abstract Expressionism and the itinerant writing as well as American popular culture which informed the second session of the Independent Group. The new ascendancy of American culture came as a result of the new Cold War situation.

# Notes

1 ICA Managing Committee Minutes, 29 April 1953, p. 4. ICA Archives.
2 ICA Managing Committee Minutes, 24 June 1953, p. 2.
3 H. Read, *Contemporary British Art*, Pelican, 1951, p. 29.
4 See course leaflet, Appendix 1.
5 L. Alloway, 'Britain's New Iron Age', *Art News* (New York), summer 1953, p. 20.
6 See Appendix 1.
7 R. Banham, 'The New Brutalism', *Architectural Review*, December 1955, p. 356.
8 B. Robertson, 'Parallel of Life and Art', *Art News and Review*, 19 September 1953.
9 R. Banham, 'The New Brutalism', *Architectural Review*, December 1955, p. 356.
10 See Appendix 1.

# 5

## Cold War culture

THE INDEPENDENT Group's reworking of modernism took place against the background of a shifting ideology in the meaning of avant-garde practice. This important shift happened between 1946 and 1956:

When, in 1946, an exhibition of American painting . . . was held at the Tate Gallery, modern American painting was perhaps regarded with a limited enthusiasm in Europe . . . in the intervening years, however, one development in American art, that which has been called abstract expressionism . . . has gained for the United States an influence upon European art which it has never exerted before.[1]

This review of the 1956 Tate Gallery exhibition, *Fifty Years of American Art* isolates one of the most significant aspects of the post-war British cultural scene. During the 1930s through to the aftermath of the Second World War, modernism signified radical European art and design. However, by 1956 the situation had dramatically altered and modernism had come to represent American achievements in avant-garde art and design. This shift in the meaning of modernism was symptomatic of the new global balance of power engendered by the Marshall Plan, which generated Britain's increased dependency, both politically and economically on the United States. As Serge Guilbaut has argued in his book, *How New York Stole the Idea of Modern Art*, the ascendancy of American culture was sustained by the United States' authorities and wealthy individuals, in an attempt to enhance the image of America throughout Europe.[2] While Guilbaut has outlined this shift in the ideology of modernism from a North American perspective, the phenomenon needs to be analysed from the British standpoint to map out its effect on the ICA and the Independent Group.

It is misleading to characterise the art of the early 1950s in terms of a polarisation between realism and abstraction. It has been argued that the major concern of the art world at this time was the debate about abstract art versus figuration.[3] However, during the early 1950s abstract art was still regarded as radical, both culturally and politically. Divisions were drawn instead between international modernism and a national school of realism. Neo-Romanticism did share some characteristics with the Kitchen Sink School – a British group of painters consisting of John Bratby, Edward Middleditch and Jack Smith which celebrated the everyday and the ordinary in realist style.[4] The two idioms were regarded as the polar opposite to the work of the continental avant-garde as supported by the ICA.

However, this polarisation was to be eclipsed in the later 1950s with the rise of American Abstract Expressionism. The transposition of the ideology of modernism during the period 1946 to 1956 was most evident in a British context at the ICA. As Herbert Read intimated to Roland Penrose in 1956 'The ICA is really the London branch of the international movement.'[5] From its foundation, the ICA enjoyed productive relations with American institutions. Roland Penrose had stored the most important works from his collection at the Museum of Modern Art, New York, during the war, thus enabling the ICA to borrow Picasso's *Les Demoiselles d'Avignon* (1906–7) from the Museum for an insurance fee of $330 for the *40,000 Years of Modern Art* exhibition. In April 1948 Nelson Rockefeller donated $2,500 to the ICA prompting Roland Penrose to write in thanks 'nothing could be nearer to our desires than to feel that we have your backing and a close relationship with the Museum of Modern Art, with whose aims and ideals we have so much in common.'[6]

When the ICA moved to Dover Street in 1950 it was still regarded as the British leader of modernism, hence the *Evening Standard* dubbed the new gallery and offices the 'Advance guard H.Q.'[7] The disappearance of Guy Burgess and Donald Maclean again linked the ICA with radical politics. Burgess and Maclean had probably joined the ICA at some point between Maclean's return from the Egyptian Embassy in May 1950 and Burgess's departure for Washington in October 1950. The two Soviet spies would have joined the ICA because of their interest in the arts and their acquaintance with the London circle which supported the Institute; Burgess also lived at 10 New Bond Street near the ICA. The ICA became connected with the political scandal after a *Daily Express* reporter, Donald Seaman, interviewed W. H. Auden and discovered that Auden, Burgess and Maclean were all members of the ICA. Through Reuters news agency this fact was communicated through every national and provincial newspaper on 11 June 1951.

Paradoxically, at the very time when the ICA was publicly linked with radical politics, American culture was making inroads into the programme of exhibitions and lectures. The exhibition, *American Symbolic Realism*, which took place during July and August 1950, was entirely financed by the American founder of the New York City Ballet, Lincoln Kirstein. He paid for the catalogue and brought the paintings over from the United States free of charge to the ICA. One of the paintings included in the exhibition, *Orthodox Boys* (1948) by Bernard Perlin, was presented to the Tate Gallery by Lincoln Kirstein through the ICA. American funds were again offered the following year through Kirstein for an exhibition of American painting. The Managing Committee was compelled to refuse, as this was Festival year and no space could be given to American art.

From 1951 to 1953 American interests were channelled into the ICA through Anthony Kloman, the brother-in-law of the Director of the Department of Architecture and Design at the Museum of Modern Art, Philip Johnson and former American cultural attaché in Europe, introduced by Roland Penrose. The appointment of Kloman as Director of Public Relations at the ICA in April 1951 signalled the point at which the balance between the old, radical, European-orientated ICA gave way to the new, ostensibly apolitical, American-orientated ICA. Kloman formed part of the highly controversial Patrick Dolan scheme, which caused a rift between Roland Penrose and George Hoellering on one side, against Herbert Read and the Arts Council on the other. Dolan, an American public relations expert, had proposed that the ICA secure a royal figurehead, possibly Princess Elizabeth, through whom funds from various large corporations could be secured for exhibitions and new premises. The Museum of Modern Art operated a similar scheme, and Penrose believed that the ICA would not suffer by following this example. However, Herbert Read was immensely critical. In an important letter to Philip James in January 1951 he wrote:

Roland is somewhat sold to the idea. I *am* very sceptical – indeed, I see the beginning of the end of any ideals I ever had for the ICA. I have said that before we take the plunge we must see whether there is any chance of a completely alternative system of support – the system represented by the Arts Council and to a lesser extent by the British Council. With the history of the MMA in mind, I do not believe that we could possibly maintain any degree of independence if we became a charitable dependency on Big Business. Dolan agrees that we cannot, in this country, expect individual support from rich patrons – it must be from 'industrial undertakings', monopolies like Lever Bros, ICI etc. I think this diagnosis is right; but it makes me all the less confident that we should be allowed to conduct the Institute as an outpost for experimental art. They might buy us up to make us socially harmless, but I don't see a lot of cunning tycoons such as Dolan associates giving immense sums of money to support an activity which they would rightly suspect of being 'subversive'.[8]

Thus, Read was still making the pre-war correlation between radical art and radical politics, a link that was to be eradicated by the rise of the American avant-garde. Philip James and the Chairman of the Arts Council, Sir Ernest Pooley, were in agreement with Read but the scheme was eventually to be accepted by the ICA. One major factor in their decision was Penrose's offer of one thousand pounds with which to launch it.

Anthony Kloman's presence at the ICA certainly led to more exhibitions from America being shown at the Institute, as well as vital dollars being made available for certain projects. During 1952 the ICA showed a collection of Saul Steinberg drawings and a series of photographs from *Life* magazine, money for the latter being pro-vided by Time–Life Incorporated. The photographs had already been shown at the Museum of Modern Art in New York, from where they were shipped still mounted, free of charge to the ICA. A lavish opening marked the exhibition of *The Old and the New in South-East Asia*, which comprised photographs by Derek Knight, and was sponsored by Shell Petroleum Company (Figure 23). Kloman was largely responsible for the Shell exhibition, which earned 150 guineas for the ICA in gallery hire fees. Previously ICA openings had been attended by 'bearded artists in duffle coats . . . sculptors in overalls and successful playwrights wearing white gardenias.'[9] However, the Shell opening, reported in the *Tatler and Bystander*, reflected the upmarket image which Kloman was attempting to create at the ICA. The opening was attended by the upper echelons of London society, including Lord Latham, Lady Gent, Lady Cator and Lord Milverton, as well as the Petroleum Attaché at the American Embassy, Mr E. Moline.

Kloman was largely responsible for the ICA's involvement with the controversial *Unknown Political Prisoner* competition, now accepted as a propaganda exercise on behalf of the CIA.[10] The competition was open to artists from any nation, who were invited to submit a maquette for judgement by an international jury. The competition was eventually won by British artist Reg Butler but never erected in full size in Berlin as was planned (Figure 24). The ICA was initially reluctant to take any part in the operation but when the amount of sponsorship involved was revealed it had little choice but to accept. The international competition was staged with £16,000 of American money, at least £1,000 of which went to the ICA as an organising fee. Those who ran the ICA were, according to Dorothy Morland, 'politically naive' at that time.[11] Read may have suspected that finance from large corporations may detract from the subversive nature of the ICA but he did not suspect that such American funding was the result of an organised attempt on behalf of the American authorities to promote Cold War ideology. It transpired much later that the £16,000 came from John Hay (Jock) Whitney, the American publisher of the *International Herald Tribune*, and Honorary Trustee of the Museum of Modern Art.[12] When subsequent discussions were taking place about the erection of the sculpture, Alfred Barr of the Museum of Modern Art, New York who was a member of the judging panel, wrote to Anthony Kloman stating:

since I gather that Penrose and Butler are not at all aware that the so-called donor's contribution was a very modest amount and that he was acting really as an anonymous front for the expenditure of funds coming from quite another source. Otherwise, the donor, who is actually known to Roland and several other people, stands in the rather awkward position of having reneged on what seems to have been a promise to see the erection of the monument through. I think you may be able to do this without naming the major source of the funds. Also, I think you could point out that the reason the 'corporate' funds were not forthcoming was the direct consequence of the British reception to the prizewinning design.[13]

Whitney was also chief financier of the successful 1952 Eisenhower/Nixon campaign and had worked for the Office of Strategic Services during the war. Whitney was also closely linked with OSS's successor, the Central Intelligence Agency (CIA), from its foundation in 1947. In 1967 it was revealed by the *New York Times* that the John Hay Whitney Charitable Trust, established in 1957, was used as a conduit for CIA funds. Whitney was also involved in the running of another CIA front, Radio Free Europe, and the CIA's Congress for Cultural Freedom. Hence, it could be claimed that the *Unknown Political Prisoner* competition was a CIA exercise in promoting liberal, individualist politics and the avant-garde.

The Russians refused to take part. Professor Valdimir Kemonov,

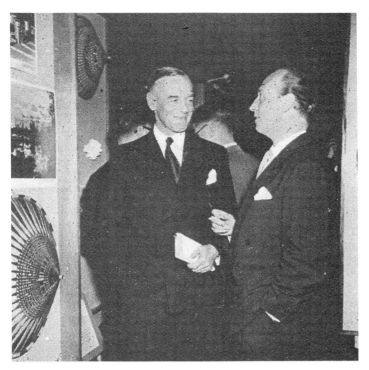

23] Opening of *The Old and the New in South-East Asia* exhibition at the ICA, 1952 showing Anthony Kloman. Published in the high society magazine *The Tatler and Bystander*

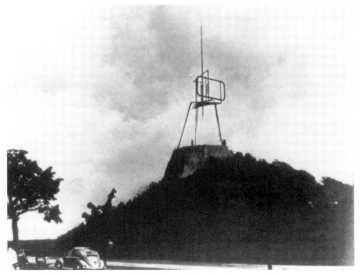

24] Reg Butler, *Monument to the Unknown Political Prisoner*, 1953. Photomontage showing sculptures superimposed on the proposed site, the Humboldt Höhe in the Wedding district near the Berlin Wall in the former western sector

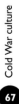

the Corresponding Member of the Academy of Arts, USSR, was invited to join the competition but refused. On 26 November 1951 he had lectured at the ICA on the *Soviet Attitude to Art* in an event organised jointly with the Society for Cultural Relations with the USSR. His refusal to take part in the competition and the failure of any Russians to submit maquettes came as a result of Soviet suspicion of the Americans' involvement. It also marks a hardening of attitudes between east and west in the Cold War. Although CIA involvement with the ICA is difficult to prove conclusively, their close involvement with *Encounter*, the European cultural journal, has been proved. Stephen Spender shared joint editorship with Irving Kristol for this magazine, sponsored by the Congress for Cultural Freedom – an organisation funded by the CIA. Spender was a member of the ICA Managing Committee from June 1953 and links between *Encounter* and the Institute flourished in the 1950s with contributions being made by Banham, Alloway, David Sylvester and Herbert Read, and the ICA Bulletin carrying advertising for the journal from December 1953 onwards.

Whilst American links with the ICA were strengthened during the 1950s, those with Russia were dropped completely owing to Cold War allegiances. After Professor Kemonov, the last Russian to speak at the ICA was film-maker, G. V. Alexandrov in November 1953. Although he was warmly thanked for his contribution, Dorothy Morland made the comment at the Managing Committee meeting of October 1953 'that if Soviet visitors in this country were invited to speak at the ICA it was unlikely that any financial help would be forthcoming from American sources'.[14] The showing of modernist art in the Eastern Bloc was similarly curtailed. For example, in 1959 an exhibition of work by Henry Moore held in Warsaw and organised by the British Council prompted allegations about the 'decadence of art in the west,' and the withdrawal of any showing of abstract painting in Poland.[15]

The ICA acted as the 'Gateway to Europe' for American high culture during the 1950s.[16] Apart from organising the *Unknown Political Prisoner* competition, the ICA showed the work of Jackson Pollock for the first time in London as a last minute addition to the *Opposing Forces* exhibition in 1953 (Figure 25). The show consisted of works by French action painters, including George Mathieu, selected by the dealer Michel Tapie. Peter Watson had discovered that the Pollock canvas, *Painting 1949*, was available for exhibition in Switzerland and included it swiftly as something of an anomaly in *Opposing Forces* some days after the show opened. There was a Mark Tobey retrospective during 1955 and an exhibition of draw-

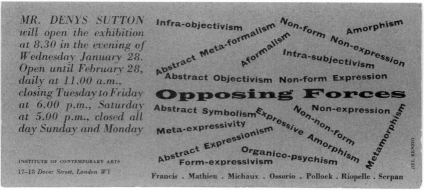

**25]** Invitation to the private view of the *Opposing Forces* exhibition, held at the ICA in 1953. Outrageous card designed by Toni del Renzio

ings from the *New Yorker*, organised by the American Federation of Arts, shown in 1956. American speakers were also welcomed at the ICA, often introduced via the American Embassy in Grosvenor Square. Most prominent included Philip Johnson who lectured on *Modern Architecture* in July 1951 and Alfred Barr Jr, then Director of Collections at the Museum of Modern Art, in March 1953. Barr was visiting London as a juror for the *Unknown Political Prisoner* competition. Barr's original title had been *Art under the Nazi and Soviet Dictatorships*, in which he proposed to voice the representative American view that Soviet Communism was as evil and destructive as Nazism, a view supported with evidence of the reactionary art of both regimes. Such an argument led to the conclusion that modern art flourished in a liberal democracy such as that of America. This was a lecture which Barr had delivered repeatedly throughout the late 1940s at various European and American venues.

Barr decided not to give the lecture after talking to Anthony Kloman:

I doubt the propriety of my talking on a subject which will seem to a lot of our English friends more American anti-communist propaganda. Since I shall be in London as a guest of the ICA and shall be involved in a competition, the subject of which is now assumed in some quarters to be American propaganda, I think it better that I withdraw.[17]

However, on Penrose's insistence, Barr did lecture on the subject of the politics of modernism, but under the alternative title of *They Hate Modern Art or Patterns of Philistine Power*. The artist Adrian Heath recalls attending the lecture, which equated liberalism in politics with modernism in art.[18]

From 1956 onwards the reputation of American painting was secured through various exhibitions in British galleries; the ICA was no longer alone in promoting American art in Britain. January 1956 marked the *Fifty Years of American Art* exhibition at the Tate Gallery. The ICA contributed to the event with two lectures by the Americans Ben Shahn and Professor Meyer Schapiro, who spoke on recent trends in American paintings at the ICA. Despite posthumous attempts to declare left-wing affinities, the Independent Group promoted American culture within the ICA, and the subsequent appointment of Lawrence Alloway as Assistant Director of the Institute ensured the continuing exposure of all things American in Dover Street. Collaboration between the American Embassy and the ICA continued in the later 1950s with the arrival of Stefan Munsing as Assistant Cultural Affairs Officer at the Embassy. Munsing participated in discussions at the ICA and made exhibitions of American art available to the Institute through the United States Information Service. The American Embassy also provided grants for Alloway and Bryan Robertson, the Director of the Whitechapel Art Gallery, to travel to the United States. In making such gestures the American authorities secured a favourable image of American culture at the avant-garde centre, namely the ICA, and elsewhere in London. From 1956 onwards New York's primacy over Paris was well-established. The British now looked to America instead of France for cultural leadership. New York had replaced Paris as the centre of modernism, and this was reflected in the second term of the Independent Group meetings during 1954 to 1955.

## Notes

1 *The Times*, 5 January 1956.

2 S. Guilbaut, *How New York Stole the Idea of Modern Art: Abstract Expressionism, Freedom and the Cold War*, University of Chicago Press, 1983.

3 D. Cherry and J. Steyn, 'The Moment of Realism 1952–1956', *Artscribe* No. 35, June 1982, pp. 44–9.

4 For more information see *The Forgotten Fifties*, exhibition catalogue, Graves Art Gallery, Sheffield, 1984.

5 H. Read, letter to Roland Penrose, 8 August 1956. Penrose Archives.

6 R. Penrose, to Nelson Rockefeller, 8 May 1948, A. H. Barr Papers, Museum of Modern Art, New York.

7 The *Evening Standard*, 6 December 1950.

8 Unpublished MS, dated 12 February 1951, Arts Council Archives.

9 *Manchester Guardian*, 12 December 1951.

10 See, for example, Richard Calvocoressi 'Public Sculpture in the 1950s' in Sandy Nairne and Nicholas Serota (eds), *British Sculpture in the Twentieth Century*,

exhibition catalogue, Whitechapel Art Gallery, 1981, and Robert Burstow, 'Butler's Competition Project for a Monument to the "Unknown Political Prisoner": Abstraction and Cold War Politics', *Art History*, Vol. 12, No. 4, December 1989, pp. 472–96.

11 Dorothy Morland interview with author, 20 August 1984.

12 Joan Edwards interviewed by Dorothy Morland, 19 June 1974, p. 4. ICA Archives.

13 Unpublished MS, letter from A. H. Barr to A. Kloman, 6 January 1955, A. H. Barr Papers, Museum of Modern Art, New York.

14 Managing Committee Minutes, 29 October 1953.

15 Unpublished MS, letter from Clive Robinson to Director, Fine Arts Dept, British Council, 17 December 1959. British Council Archives.

16 ICA Memo, 'American Culture and the Institute of Contemporary Arts', 1957. ICA Archives.

17 Unpublished MS, dated 2 February 1953. ICA Archives.

18 Adrian Heath interview with author, 7 January 1984.

# The Expendable Aesthetic and America

THE EXPENDABLE Aesthetic was the most important contribution which the Independent Group made to a revisionist understanding of cultural values. The concept that style was not timeless directly challenged orthodox modernism as did the levelling of mass and high culture. It was during the second phase of the Independent Group, from 1954 to 1955, that earlier preoccupations with overturning the assumptions of modernism were incorporated with a serious analysis of American mass culture using largely American sources to propose the theory of the Expendable Aesthetic. This chapter will explore and analyse the sources of the Expendable Aesthetic.

The Independent Group did not meet formally during 1953 to 1954 as members were involved with the *Aesthetic Problems of Contemporary Art* programme and contributing to the general running of the ICA. More lectures were given by Group members to the ICA public. Banham remained on the Managing Committee on Herbert Read's return from America whilst Lawrence Alloway replaced Toni del Renzio on the Exhibitions Sub-Committee. The reputations of Eduardo Paolozzi and William Turnbull had been enhanced by their participation in the Venice Biennale during 1953. Paolozzi was also one of the five sculptors selected to represent Great Britain in the *Unknown Political Prisoner* competition, for which he was awarded an Arts Council prize. Paolozzi and Turnbull were also two of twenty-eight artists to be commissioned to design textile prints by *Ambassador*, a British export magazine, which were exhibited at the ICA. Paolozzi was also included in the ICA exhibition *Recent British Drawing*, a selection of work made by David Sylvester.

As the artistic careers of the various Group members became more established, so personal rivalries and schisms began to emerge. The manner in which Lawrence Alloway replaced Toni del Renzio on the Exhibitions Sub-Committee is indicative of the nature of the often strained relationships between Group members. In a meeting of the Managing Committee Banham objected to the introduction to the *Parallel of Life and Art* exhibition catalogue written by Toni del Renzio which 'was liable to make the organisers of the exhibition look ridiculous.'[1] Del Renzio's inflammatory piece was withdrawn and he resigned from the Exhibitions Sub-Committee. He was replaced by Lawrence Alloway on 9 October 1953. Alloway exploited his position to mount various exhibitions, beginning with the work of Victor Pasmore. Lawrence Alloway also succeeded Reyner Banham as convenor of the Independent Group in the autumn of 1954 and the Group presented a public lecture series entitled *Books and the Modern Movement*, chaired by Banham.

Running from October to December 1954, the series of five lectures considered the contribution of key texts to the understanding of modernism in Britain. Attended by a small audience, the series marked a crucial stage in the Group's revision of modernism. Alloway's discussion of Herbert Read's *Art Now* drew on the critique he had made of Read in his book, *Nine Abstract Artists* (1954):

Read observed that 'the work of art that can express such a transcendental quality must of necessity be far removed from the mundane world of actual appearances'. There the platonic drift of abstract aesthetics is summed up: geometry is the means to a higher world.[2]

Alloway strove to rid the theory of abstract art of 'These obstinate absolutes'[3] by rejecting a metaphysical analysis of painting, and attempting to replace this with a more formal analysis, much in the manner that American critics, particularly Clement Greenberg, were beginning to do. The remainder of the Group was equally critical of Read. Toni del Renzio recalled: 'Our objections were primarily concerned with a certain academicising "purism" which somehow separated art from life and spoke about "harmony" while already we had recognised in Rosenburg something of the view we took of art.'[4] Banham criticised Read's 'innocent eye' approach to artistic creation, arguing instead for 'a trained – a sophisticated – eye.'[5] The division between Read's aesthetic theories and those of the Group also informed the ICA symposium on the recently published *Pedagogical Sketchbook* in November 1953. Banham reviewed the symposium and a follow up debate which took place one month later around the motion 'That the late work of Paul Klee represents a decline in his powers'. The review was published in *Encounter* and clarifies a difference of view between different age groups of British artists:

The symposium was a revealing affair, for it indicated the particular grounds on which the younger generation base their admiration of Klee, and the manner in which these differed from the grounds of an older generation of admirers.[6]

The older generation in question was represented by H. S. Williamson, Principal of Chelsea School of Art and Quentin Bell, lecturer in Art Education at the University of Durham. The younger generation was represented by those connected with the Independent Group: Lawrence Alloway and Victor Pasmore, then head of Painting at King's College in Newcastle, part of the University of Durham.

The division of opinion between the older and younger generations was clearly delineated, for Banham, by outdated academicism: 'Unlike Pasmore and Alloway, the objectors (Bell and Williamson) demanded a cut-and-dried academic text-book'.[7] Banham located this need for an art education without ambiguity within a tradition stretching back to Tonks at the Slade. Banham correlated the academic tradition of art education with a similar tendency in criticism:

Thus, from Roger Fry, who believed that form could be *ipso facto* significant, to Herbert Read, who believes the laws of beauty to be absolute and permanent, English progressive criticism has been profoundly academic.[8]

Banham and the Independent Group as a whole always eschewed their predecessors' need to establish permanent rules and values, a need characterised in this instance by the term 'academic'. The Independent Group valued Klee's treatise on teaching as it embodied an empirical and fluid approach:

But Klee's work is a live influence on a whole generation now reaching or enjoying artistic maturity, a generation to whom his symbols are anything but remote, and in the recent Seminars on Aesthetic Problems at the ICA he has been probably the most quoted source, followed – very characteristically – by the Futurist Boccioni, and contrasted against Alberti, the foundation academic.[9]

Not only did Klee's philosophy act as a liberating force for the Independent Group's formulation of a new and more dynamic aesthetic, but also the visual symbols he used entered into the paintings of the Group. Section Four of Klee's *Pedagogical Sketchbook*, 'Symbols of Form in Motion', had an important impact on Richard Hamilton's work at the time. The *Trainsition* series of four paintings features a key symbol from the work of Klee – the arrow. As Banham observed, 'Symbols of Form in Motion' was 'a sort of apotheosis of Klee's favourite symbol, the arrow.'[10] The arrow features as a significant symbolic device in the four *Trainsition* works. They deal with the problem of representing movement on a static, two-dimensional surface. At the time, Hamilton was frequently travelling to Newcastle upon Tyne by train to teach at King's College. In *Trainsition IIII* (Figure 26) Hamilton describes the view from the speeding train window on to the disappearing landscape. The surface of the canvas is covered with delicate, subtle brushstrokes, representing the blurred view from the window of the world outside. The movement of the train is represented by the large, black arrow at the base of the painting, the movement of the car near the top of the canvas is indicated by a smaller arrow, and the constantly shifting landscape by an even

**26]** Richard Hamilton, *Trainsition IIII* (1954). Oil on canvas, 91.5 x. 122 cm. Given by Richard Hamilton to his son Roderic Hamilton, presented by him to the Tate Gallery

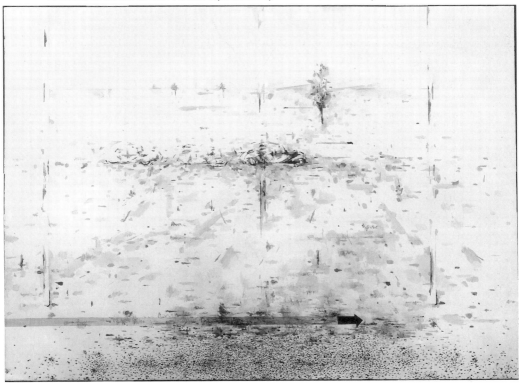

smaller arrow further up the painting. *Trainsition III* represents the same scenario only depicted from the front of the train with two large arrows diagrammatically representing the forward thrust of the engine.

It has been suggested that the title for the *Trainsition* series derived from an anagram of 'Train I sit on'.[11] It was also claimed at the time by Alloway that the paintings referred to a typical situation in Hollywood movies of the car chase.[12] However, as is frequently the case with the works of the Independent Group, references to modernism are occluded in their subsequent analysis. *Transition* was the title of an important avant-garde magazine published during the inter-war years which strongly featured Surrealist writing. An anthology of *Transition* articles was published in New York in 1949 under the title *Transition Workshop*. Significantly the inside front page of the book carries an arrow. Hamilton would have known of the magazine through his Surrealist connections and interests in James Joyce. A post-war successor was published entitled *Transition Forty-Eight*, edited by Georges Duthuit and carrying writing by André Malraux, André Breton, Antonin Artaud, Samuel Beckett and Jean-Paul Sartre. The series of *Trainsition* paintings may well have referred to Hollywood films but it should also be taken into account that there are references to Paul Klee, Siegfried Giedion and *Transition* magazine. As is frequently the case with the analysis of work by the Independent Group, any references which connect forward to the creation of Pop Art are emphasised and references to modernism marginalised.

The *Trainsition* paintings were included in Richard Hamilton's first solo show at the Hanover Gallery in January 1955. They also provided the focus for the first meeting of the 1954/55 session of the Independent Group on 11 February 1955. Banham utilised the material covered in his review of the Hamilton exhibition for *Art* magazine of January 1955 in his subsequent discussion of the works. As no detailed records were kept of the Group's discussions, an indication of their content can be gleaned through members' publications. Banham proposed that Hamilton's work was both a critique of Slade School and Soviet Realism, as well as the accepted view of modernism in Britain held by the Neo-Romantics. Banham put forward the notion that Hamilton's work constituted a serious re-evaluation of modernism:

Each picture requires close and imaginative attention, for these are – almost uniquely in contemporary English art – genuinely intellectual paintings, the product of directed cerebration.[13]

The decision to reconvene the Independent Group seems to have been made by Dorothy Morland. Banham was now concentrating full-time on his Ph.D. thesis at the Courtauld, and so was unable to act again as convenor. John McHale recalled being approached by Morland, and asked if he would act as convenor. John McHale had attended the end of the first series of Independent Group lectures with Lawrence Alloway, whom he had met at art history classes at the Courtauld Institute of Art and he was enthusiastic about the Group's project of 'demolishing history'.[14]

The second session of the Group focused on American mass culture. The Group certainly admired American high culture and this enthusiasm was easily linked with an analysis of 'low' culture as Alloway observed:

I felt that the painting I liked and the mass media product which I liked the best was coming from the United States rather than the accustomed source in Europe. So that linked – it was natural, therefore – to like Hollywood and Jackson Pollock.[15]

To Alloway a serious analysis of American mass culture was a continuation of the concerns of the first session, where American mass-produced objects and images were at the cutting edge of technological progress: 'when the cars were bigger and the tail fins higher and the camera work was getting more mobile, the colour was better and the screen was bigger.'[16] The Independent Group did not share the enthusiasm of some scholars for traditional British popular culture which had emerged during the Festival of Britain year. The Group distinguished between traditional, craft based popular culture and the new, mass culture by the use of the term 'pop art'.

Mass culture was certainly an unusual topic of interest for a collection of artists, architects and art historians to be engaged with in the early 1950s. *Parade of Pleasure: A Study of Popular Iconography in the USA* (1954) by Geoffrey Wagner is typical of the criticism which American mass culture attracted during this period in Britain. Wagner examined American 'movies', television, the pin-up and comic books and found them to be in poor taste and a source of corruption for the young. Indeed, the American comic books which the Independent Group avidly discussed and collected were the subject of such widespread criticism that some were actually banned from import under the Children and Young Persons (Harmful Publications) Act of 1955. Such an interest certainly acted as a challenge to Herbert Read, whose approach Alloway accurately summarised:

he was committed to the idealistic aesthetic in which high tasks were assumed to be proper for art and so much got neglected and so, on that basis the mass production methods were a way of opposing Sir Herbert. There was nobody much else to attack.[17]

Read himself was a frequent visitor to the United States during the 1950s but deplored the development there of an all pervasive, consumer culture. He wrote to Howard Newby of the BBC in 1951:

This is my fourth visit to America, so I am no longer excited about skyscrapers, American women, or even American automobiles. The enduring satisfactions are American plumbing, unlimited supplies of orange-juice and the telephone operators . . . The new horror is the undergraduate in tight jeans with 'crew-cropped' head and ape-like slouch. Thousands of them, identical.[18]

Alloway introduced the subject of mass culture into the ICA's programme of talks before the Independent Group reconvened in February 1955. On 19 January 1954 he lectured on 'Science Fiction' and on 1 July he and Toni del Renzio gave a public dialogue on the Western film genre. The ICA's founders had always considered film to be part of their area of responsibility in the promotion of avant-garde practice in general. Hence they organised regular screenings of European 'art' films at the French Institute. During 1954 these included *Guernica* (1949–50, directed by Alain Resnais and Robert Hassens), *Le Grand Meulnes* (1953, directed by Georges Franju) and *Die Dreigroschenoper* (1931, directed by G. W. Pabst). The nature of the film programme at the ICA was determined by the overall cultural view of the Managing Committee, by which painting represented the pinnacle of cultural achievement which other arts attempted to emulate. This approach to cinema was directly challenged by Lawrence Alloway at the end of 1954, when a series of illustrated talks he had arranged was announced in the ICA *Bulletin* in December 1954:

The material will be controversial, and will not necessarily represent the views of the ICA Film Sub-Committee. He writes 'There is a tendency to regard cinema as a great art form which has been ruined by popularity and commercialism. Critics of the cinema set up ideals and principles, usually derived from the silent film, and on this basis look for the Ten Best Films of the Year. It is proposed to arrange a series of meetings on cinema which does not treat the film as an art form manqué but as a modern popular art. These meetings will deal with the currency of the movies, not with hypothetical absolutes.'

The series of talks was announced as not being entirely representative of the ICA's Film Sub-Committee as it was stated in a meeting of the Managing Committee that:

a majority of the Film Sub-Committee were in favour of Lawrence Alloway's scheme. However, both Mr Forman and Mr Read felt that the scheme needed considerable modification before it should be accepted by the ICA. Mr Alloway, on the other hand, said he was not prepared to proceed with the series unless he was allowed to conduct it entirely as he thought best.[19]

A compromise was reached as the programme of four talks ran as Alloway had proposed. The series opened in February 1955 with a lecture by Carl Foreman, the scriptwriter of *High Noon* and *Crossfire* describing 'Post-War American Memories'. The author of *The Technique of Film Editing*, Karl Reisz, gave the second talk in the series on 'Recent American Movies in Europe'. The third event of the series was a 'Symposium on Film Heroines' and involved Toni del Renzio discussing Audrey Hepburn, and David Sylvester lecturing on Marilyn Monroe under the chairmanship of Alloway. The series concluded with Alloway speaking on 'The Movies as a Mass Medium' – again, challenging orthodox modernist views of film. Preferring movies to films, the Group attempted a serious analysis of Hollywood, using the tools of non-Aristotelian logic. The adoption of such a philosophy allowed the Group to form a serious view of what was the most popular cinema in post-war Britain. From the established standpoint such films could not be considered seriously as they were not art. The non-Aristotelian standpoint allowed the Group to examine the complex mythology, structure and role-playing evident in popular cinema. Therefore, the Independent Group was involved in the decoding of cultural artefacts, rather than ascertaining which were bad and which good.

Not only was the Independent Group augmented by Alloway and McHale, but also Alison and Peter Smithson. The Smithsons had been involved with the *Parallel of Life and Art* exhibition with Paolozzi and Henderson at the ICA and would have been introduced to the Independent Group by this means. This also explains the reason for the Smithsons, Henderson and Paolozzi forming something of a 'splinter group'. Alison Smithson distinguished this smaller group from the remainder, whom she termed the 'grey men', meaning the theoreticians such as Banham, del Renzio and Alloway.[20] Another sub-group was formed by the addition of a musical director from EMI, Frank Cordell and his wife, a Hungarian abstract painter, Magda Cordell. The Cordells, Lawrence Alloway and John McHale, whom Magda was subsequently to live with in America, formed this second splinter group. Magda Cordell was to exhibit her collages and monotypes at an ICA exhibition in the summer of 1955 whilst her Pollock-inspired canvases were shown at

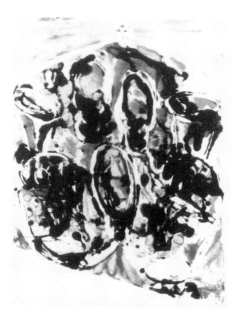

**27]** Magda Cordell, *Untitled* (1954–55). Monoprint, red, black and yellow paint on paper, printed from a broken marble slab, collection of the artist

the Hanover Gallery in a solo show in the winter of 1956 (Figure 27). In the catalogue introduction for the latter, Lawrence Alloway was to describe her work in terms of a list of science-fiction key words, including: 'solar, delta, galactic, amorphous, ulterior, fused, far out, viscous, . . . hyper-space, free fall.'[21]

The nucleus formed by Paolozzi, Mary and Peter Reyner Banham, Magda and Frank Cordell, Alloway, Toni del Renzio, Richard and Terry Hamilton, William Turnbull, the Smithsons and Nigel Henderson was constantly augmented by various peripheral visitors. Dorothy Morland, Victor Pasmore, Sam Stevens, Colin St John Wilson, Theo Crosby, Anthony Hill, Richard Smith, Roger Coleman, Patrick Heron, James Stirling, Kenneth and Mary Martin were amongst those who would very occasionally attend one of the monthly meetings. Others were aware of the Independent Group's functioning, for example, the abstract artist Adrian Heath, but never attended a meeting because they were not invited or because they did not share the Group's enthusiasm for American culture.

Not only was the second session of the Independent Group different from the first in scope and membership, but also in format. The purpose of the meetings was no longer to gather and hear the word of the outside expert. Because mass culture was the chief point of interest for the Group, there seemed to be no specialists equipped to address meetings. The one exception to this apart from Meyer was

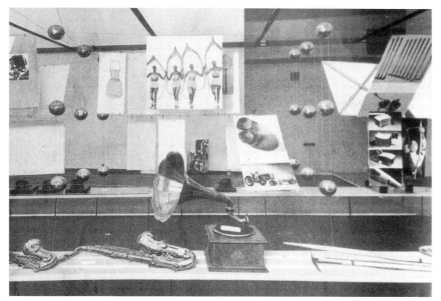

28] The industrial design display at the Tenth Milan Triennale in 1954. Designed by Portles, Russell and Zanuso

the Italian design critic and theorist, Gillo Dorfles. Dorfles had spoken at the ICA on 21 May 1953 about 'The Contemporary Point of View of the Baroque'. Apparently the lecture had not attracted a large audience, and when the ICA management was informed that Dorfles was visiting London again in June 1955 for the exhibition of Italian Industrial Design at the Italian Institute, Belgrave Square, the Independent Group was told and a meeting arranged. According to Banham, Dorfles spoke on the 'Aesthetics of Product Design'. Dorfles had worked with the editor of the leading design magazine *Stile Industria*, Alberto Rosselli and major designer Marco Zanuso on the industrial design section at the Tenth Triennale in 1954 – Italy's major design exhibition. This polemical display of fridges, musical instruments and vacuum cleaners sought to bridge the gap between product design and fine art, between fantasy and function, as did the international conference which accompanied the exhibition (Figure 28). This anti-absolutist approach reinforced the Independent Group's re-evaluation of modernism and their erosion of barriers between art and design.

This was a perspective which Banham adopted for his contribution to this Independent Group session entitled 'Borax, or the Thousand Horse-Power Mink' on 4 March 1955. Analysing contemporary images of car styling taken from American advertising, Banham applied the Surrealist concept of fantasy and dream

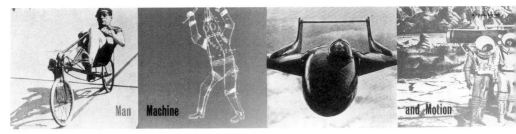

Man Machine and Motion

**29]** Invitation to the opening of the *Man, Machine and Motion* exhibition held at the ICA in 1955

fulfilment to these all-American products. Sexual symbolism was a second theme to be explored. Banham asserted in his article, 'Machine Aesthetic', that it was by means of the 'symbolic content' that car styling could be analysed.[22] Banham's introduction of iconology to the reading of industrial design had repercussions for Richard Hamilton, not only for his painting, but also for his teaching and exhibition work. During 1955 Hamilton organised with Banham the *Man, Machine and Motion* exhibition which was shown at the ICA during July (Figures 29 and 30). The exhibition dealt with themes which had been common currency throughout the lifespan of the Independent Group. The blown up photographs and diagrams illustrating the technical evolution of human mobility, echoed the Group's concern with arriving at new means of cultural

**30]** Installation shot of *Man, Machine and Motion* as it appeared at the Hatton Gallery, University of Newcastle in 1955

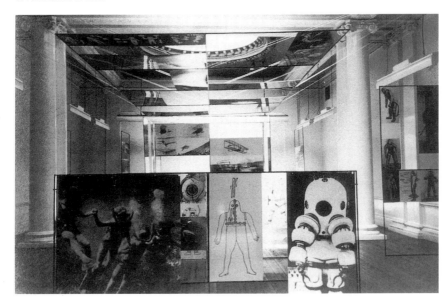

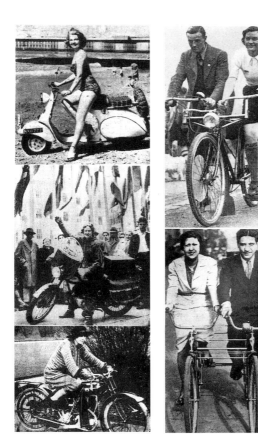

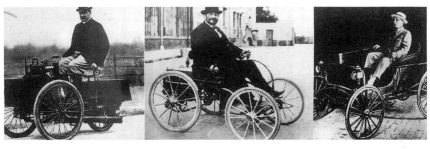

31,32] Panels from the *Man, Machine and Motion* exhibition, Hatton Gallery at Newcastle

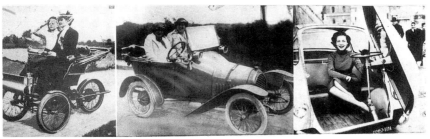

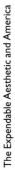

analysis. The majority of the photographs represented people interacting with machinery designed for transport (Figures 31 and 32). Lawrence Gowing, the Head of Fine Art at King's College, Newcastle, where Hamilton was now lecturing and which housed the first showing of *Man, Machine and Motion* was doubtful about the content of the show. He confided to Roland Penrose:

We have not yet quite decided how far we can shoulder the costs which he (Richard Hamilton) envisages, and I have myself not decided whether the rather limited theme in which he is interested can be said to fall within the province of our gallery without the addition of a certain amount of material of a more general artistic character. However, Richard is evidently determined to persevere with his plans.[23]

Gowing's attitude to *Man, Machine and Motion* reflects the established view of what could safely be considered as appropriate material for an exhibition, namely fine art. In this respect Hamilton and the Independent Group were challenging accepted values, just as Alloway had with his series of film lectures.

The remainder of the Independent Group meetings during 1955 consisted of one member speaking on a particular aspect of mass culture, or general discussions: Frank Cordell on 'Gold Pan Alley' in September, Toni del Renzio on 'Fashion and Fashion Magazines' in June and Richard Hamilton on domestic appliances. General discussions covered advertising during two sessions in April and May. Here again the Group thought that the best examples of advertising were coming from America. Just as Cinemascope had been developed in America, so the most advanced forms of colour printing could be seen in American periodicals. In comparison to *Life, McCalls, Scientific American* and *National Geographic*, British counterparts were lacking in terms of technique and graphic design (Figures 33 and 34). As Banham recalled:

One of the great trainings for the public's eye was reading American magazines. We goggled at the graphics and the colour-work in adverts for appliances that were almost inconceivable in power-short Britain, and food ads so luscious you wanted to eat them. Remember we had spent our teenage years surviving the horrors and deprivations of a six-year war. For us, the fruits of peace had to be tangible, preferably edible. Those ads may look yucky now, to the overfed eyes of today, but to us they looked like Paradise Regained – or at least a paper promise of it.[24]

Whilst this aspect of the Group's interest in American advertising should not be overlooked, it had tended to provide the only explanation for their interest. Not only did the Group examine American advertising because unattainable goods were lucidly illustrated in them, but because the adverts drew upon a sophisticated code which they sought to deconstruct: a code which formed part of the game operating between the consumer and creator of the image. Because the meetings now consisted of the members addressing one another, rather than outsiders coming in, they were far more informal and discussions were not confined to the meetings; they would continue in Soho pubs and members' houses. It was during these frequent and informal discussions amongst the nucleus of the Independent Group during 1955 that the notion of an Expendable Aesthetic was formulated. The Group had formed a critical awareness of the philosophy of modernism during its first session, using the latest advances in technology as a critique. Now the foundation of the Group's critique of modernism was extended with the analysis of mass culture. The Group used American sources to interpret such material. This interpretation led to the proposal of a new, broad-based aesthetic.

The Group was familiar with the philosophy of British Empiricism, particularly the work of A. J. Ayer and D'Arcy Wentworth Thompson. It was Lawrence Alloway who introduced contemporary American philosophy into the Independent Group's discussions, as he recalled:

this thing about non-Aristotelian logic and so forth, I got it from A. E. Van Vogt's *The World of Null-A* . . . and I read a bit of Korzybski . . . and I liked very much consciously the notion of getting it from slightly disreputable science fiction – I say disreputable because the science fiction people don't really approve of A. E. Van Vogt, and applying this to the area of the fine arts.[25]

Alloway discovered the concept of non-Aristotelian logic through his reading of A. E. Van Vogt in post-war science fiction magazines such as *Astounding Science Fiction* which came from America (Figure 35). Published in book form in 1948 in America and 1970 in Britain, *The World of Null-A* does not display any serious attempt to come to terms with non-Aristotelian logic. However, there are references to Korzybski, with quotes from *Science and Sanity* opening every chapter and the action taking place around the Semantics building. Alloway's reading of Van Vogt led to the source book on non-Aristotelian logic, A. C. Korzybski's *Science and Sanity: An Introduction to Non-Aristotelian Systems and General Semantics* (1933). It is doubtful whether the Independent Group studied this eight hundred-page tome in any depth, particularly chapters such as 'Semantics of the Differential Calculus' or 'Semantics of the Einstein Theory'. However, the key theme within the work which

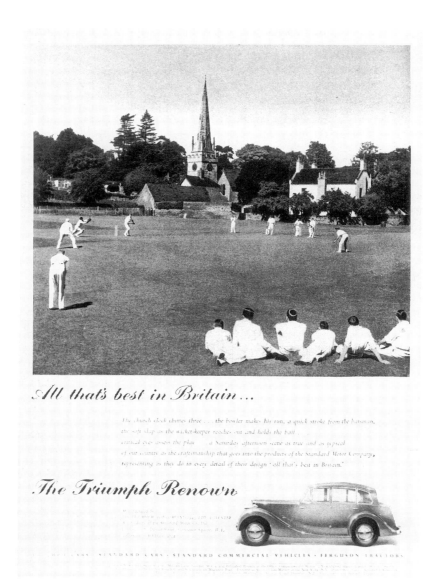

All that's best in Britain...

The Triumph Renown

**33]** British advert for the Triumph Renown, 1951

the Independent Group was certainly familiar with was that of the bankruptcy of Aristotelian philosophy.

In the preface to *Science and Sanity* Korzybski stressed that despite the technically advanced state of society, the habits of thought, language, assumptions and fundamental philosophy had not changed since the era of Aristotle. In the same manner as the Independent Group criticised the modern movement, Korzybski located the inadequacy of Aristotelian thought within

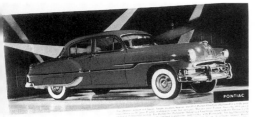

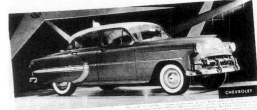

Masterworks of Craftsmanship . . .   Masterpieces of Engineering . . .

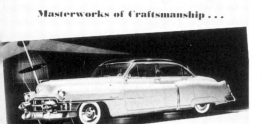

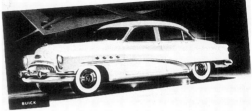

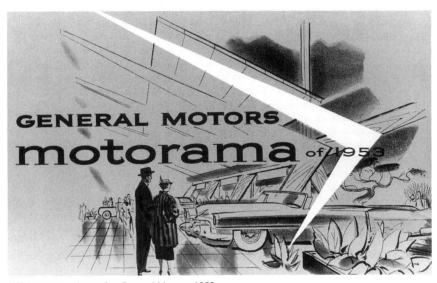

**34]** American adverts for General Motors, 1953

its reliance upon metaphysics. Ozenfant's *Foundations of Modern Art* (1931) is one example of modernist writing which the Group criticised for its Aristotelian basis. Ozenfant described Purism thus:

> But what strikes me . . . is not how ephemeral all this is, but particularly how prodigiously stable mankind is, and the common qualities that characterise everything that everywhere and at all times has profoundly affected him. These vast 'constants'. I call it 'Purism'.[26]

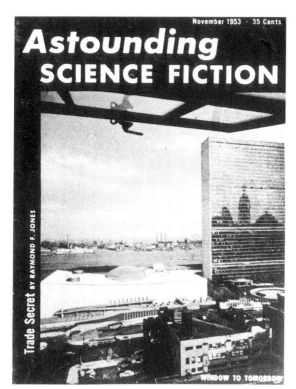

November 1953 · 35 Cents

# *Astounding*
# SCIENCE FICTION

Trade Secret BY RAYMOND F. JONES

WINDOW TO TOMORROW

**35]** Cover of *Astounding Science Fiction*, one of the foremost
publications of the genre, November 1953

The Independent Group lodged its critique of such expressions of
Aristotelian philosophy within the terms of the constantly changing nature of technology. Korzybski operated a similar critique of
language. Because the underlying structure of language is metaphysical, just as the underpinnings of modernism are metaphysical,
it is inherently Aristotelian. Korzybski prised apart the signifier
and the signified, claiming that the links between the two were
always arbitrary.

The concept of non-Aristotelian logic, of no either/or and no
natural links between signs and their meanings, liberated the
Independent Group from pre-existing assumptions about cultural
values and readings. Richard Hamilton has described the link
between non-Aristotelian logic and his painting:

the notion that you couldn't say that something was good or bad leads
to the possibility of inclusion into painting of figurative matter which
wouldn't have been conceivable without that fundamental notion of non-
Aristotelian thinking.

It gave us a very respectable base for rejection and iconoclasm to say
that American universities were now putting this forward as a very serious

and well established scientific study. The question of value judgements became so liberating that we were able to say everything we can think of is right and can be used.[27]

The introduction of non-Aristotelian thinking into Group discussions therefore led to a major revision of previous philosophies of culture. From this starting point the Group built up the notion of an Expendable Aesthetic, drawing upon other American sources.

One area of American writing which fascinated the Independent Group was that of new roles in society. The Independent Group argued that post-war British society was being radically restructured by new technology – particularly the mass media and mass production of consumer goods. As far as the Independent Group was concerned, the Council of Industrial Design's efforts to inculcate the public with a criterion of good and bad taste, based on modernist principles, were no longer relevant. The Group proposed that the chief determinants of style were the mass market and technology, and it was the task of the industrial designer to respond to both. The origin of this concept lies in an American sociology publication, David Riesman's *The Lonely Crowd* (1950). Riesman, a follower of Thorstein Veblen – author of the first full analysis of consumption, *Theory of the Leisure Class* (1899) – sought to describe the change in American society caused by 'a shift from an age of production to an age of consumption.'[28] The consumers in this new era were more perceptive and knowledgeable than ever before as increased automation led to more leisure time. As a result, the quality of popular culture improved and the quantity multiplied. According to Riesman, the post-war era was that of the autonomous consumer whose freedom of choice enabled crucial feedback to the designer and manufacturer. Freedom of choice came as a result of the increased spending power of most Americans; the manufacturer utilised market research to gauge what consumer demands were. Banham referred to this in his seminal article of 1955, 'The Machine Aesthetic':

When the American Ford Company issued a questionnaire to discover what qualities buyers sought in cars, most answerers headed their lists with such utilitarian considerations as road-holding and fuel consumption – a result which sales-analysis did not support – but when asked what *other people* looked for most people headed their lists with chromium plate, colour-schemes and so forth.[29]

Hence, industrial designers were being called on to satisfy the consumer's desire for social status by means of mass-produced objects. Both Riesman and the Independent Group naively supposed that everyone could attain the social status to which they aspired. According to Riesman the new consumer:

knows the rich man's car is only marginally, if at all, different from his own – a matter at best of a few additional horsepower. He knows anyway that next year's model will be better than this year's.[30]

The Independent Group was confident, as was the majority of British society at this time, that science and technology could only progress to bigger and better things. Banham characterised the 1950s as the 'Jet Age, the Detergent Decade, the Second Industrial Revolution.'[31] The Independent Group shared a populist view of progress and consumption, a view which presumed that an interaction between consumer and manufacturer governed style. Linked with the Group's revision of the relationship between designer and consumer was its interest in the new profession of marketing. The source material again was American, this time A. C. Spectorsky's *The Exurbanites* (1955). Spectorsky defined a new class of professional in his book:

These people, God save us all, set the styles, mould the fashions, and populate the dreams of the rest of the country. What they do will be done, a few weeks or months later, by their counterparts in Lake Forest and Santa Barbara and on the main line. What they decree, via such esoteric channels as the 'People are Talking About . . .' feature in *Vogue* will all too often be picked up and actually talked about, in Beverly Hills, Grosse Pointe, and Sewickley.[32]

The relationship between this new type of expert, who worked in the field of mass media or marketing, and the consumer was not one of exploiter and exploited. Communication between the two was vital as the consumer was becoming increasingly sophisticated and discriminating, so those attempting to sell the commodities needed to take account of feedback and tastes. The Independent Group tended to view this relationship as a game in which two equally sophisticated sides engaged in a contest of 'symbol-manipulation'[33] and symbol interpretation. Reyner Banham alluded to the intricacies of such a relationship in 'The Atavism of the Short-Distance Mini-Cyclist':

There is a great deal of evidence available to suggest that whatever the intentions of the entertainment industry, the public is not being, and apparently *cannot* be, manipulated.[34]

For Banham and the Independent Group the consumer was not the passive recipient of whatever popular culture was foisted upon them, but played an active part in the process.

Because the Independent Group perceived popular culture to be of such a complex nature, it formed part of the overall continuum of culture which the Group proposed. The concept of a continuum derived from yet another American source: in this instance it was the newly emerging discipline of cybernetics which interested the Group. This was defined by its founders, Norbert Wiener and Arturo Rosenbleuth in 1947 as 'the science of control and communication in the animal and the machine'. Wiener's seminal book on the subject, *The Human Use of Human Beings* (1950) identified and explained the science of messages. The Independent Group certainly knew of Wiener's work, and attempted to apply his communication models to visual culture. John McHale invited a British expert on cybernetics to address the Group for the third meeting in March 1955. This was E. W. Meyer, who was working on particle counters for the National Coal Board and spoke on 'Probability and Information Theory and Their Application to the Visual Arts', as McHale recalled:

We wanted somebody to do it, we found the expert to do it. Then we listened to him and realised, of course, what he was saying wouldn't make any sense whatsoever to the Group. We decided in some way to debrief him, listen to him on it, write down the ideas and try to make a set of diagrams to translate the ideas.

We had a standard Shannon diagram, then we had an example of coding, all laid out, we had a statistical probability . . . I think there were five sets of diagrams.[35]

During 1954 McHale produced a series of collages and constructions on the theme of the transistor, a recent invention which had revolutionised the world of communications (Figure 36). McHale represented the processing of information in visual form inspired by the new analysis of communication. Apart from abstract collages McHale produced scrapbooks containing images largely taken from magazines and newspapers cut into horizontal strips so that the viewer could mix and match the images as desired. The collages were exhibited in the *Collages and Objects* exhibition, organised by Lawrence Alloway late in 1954.

Therefore, in their second full session the Independent Group adopted a non-Aristotelian approach to culture, which meant that the hierarchical criterion which determined value was dismissed. The material which the Group drew upon to establish a new aesthetic was wide and varied. Non-Aristotelian logic, American sociology and cybernetics were three sources which enabled the Group to develop a new, critical approach to culture. Such sources were imaginatively combined with more traditional methodologies. For

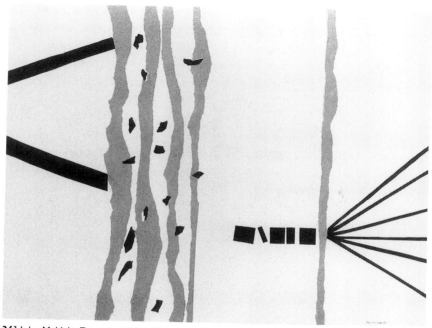

**36]** John McHale, *Transistor* (1954). Collage with black-printed paper and blue construction paper on buff ground. Image based on the Shannon Communication diagram

example the theory of iconology, then current at the Courtauld Institute of Art, was used by Banham in the analysis of car styling. In his seminal article, 'Vehicles of Desire' published in September 1955, Banham launched a full-scale attack on Platonic values and their continued currency:

We eagerly consume noisy ephemeridae, here with a bang today, gone without a whimper tomorrow – movies, beach-wear, pulp magazines, this morning's headlines and tomorrow's T. V. programmes – yet we insist on aesthetic and moral standards hitched to permanency, durability and perennity.[36]

The Expendable Aesthetic, as proposed by Banham and the rest of the Independent Group, was a radical challenge to modernism in its recognition of the constantly changing nature of style. Fashion and popular taste were not belittled by the Group but analysed seriously. The longevity of a design was no guarantee of quality. The Group proposed that consumer demand, changing technology and taste led to an Expendable Aesthetic. An American car of 1955 could be analysed symbolically in terms of its various referents but its appeal could last only five years at the most before it was supplanted by another style. The Group rejected Le Corbusier's notion, as proposed in *Vers une architecture* (1926), that the Parthenon was like a Bignan-Sport because of its timeless, classical qualities. To Banham, this hand-built, luxury car of the 1920s looked dated and was technologically obsolete.

## Notes

**1** ICA Management Committee Minutes, 18 August 1953, p. 3.

**2** L. Alloway, *Nine Abstract Artists*, Alec Tiranti Ltd., 1954, p. 1.

**3** *Ibid.*, p. 4.

**4** Toni del Renzio, 'Pioneers and Trendies', *Art and Artists*, February 1984, p. 27.

**5** R. Banham, *Fathers of Pop*, revised draft script, p. 4.

**6** R. Banham, 'Klee's Pedagogical Sketchbook', *Encounter*, April 1954, p. 53.

**7** *Ibid.*, p. 56.

**8** *Ibid.*, p. 56.

**9** *Ibid.*, p. 57.

**10** *Ibid.*, p. 54.

**11** Tate Gallery, *Modern British Paintings, Drawings and Sculpture*, Oldbourne, 1964, p. 102 also Tate Gallery, *Richard Hamilton*, catalogue of an exhibition, 1992, p. 146.

**12** L. Alloway, 'Re-Vision', *Art News and Review*, 22 January 1955, p. 5.

**13** R. Banham, 'Vision in Motion', *Art*, 5 January 1955, p. 3.

**14** John McHale, *Fathers of Pop*, discussion between John McHale, Mary and Reyner Banham and Magda Cordell, pp. 29–30.

**15** L. Alloway, interview with Reyner Banham for *Fathers of Pop*, p. 18a.

**16** *Ibid.*, pp. 3–4.

**17** *Ibid.*, p. 5.

**18** H. Read, unpublished MS dated 24 October 1951, BBC Written Archives.

**19** ICA Managing Committee Minutes, 6 October 1954, p. 4.

**20** Alison Smithson, interview with author 16 September 1983.

**21** L. Alloway, introduction to catalogue of an exhibition, *Magda Cordell Paintings*, Hanover Gallery, 1956. Unpaginated.

**22** R. Banham, 'Machine Aesthetic', *Architectural Review*, April 1955, pp. 225–8.

**23** L. Gowing, unpublished MS dated 9 June 1954, Collection University of Newcastle.

**24** R. Banham, *Fathers of Pop*, revised draft script, p. 5.

**25** L. Alloway, *Fathers of Pop*, interview with Banham, p. 10.

**26** A. Ozenfant, *The Foundations of Modern Art*, Dover Publications, New York, 1952, p. xiii. First published in English in 1931.

**27** R. Hamilton, *Fathers of Pop*, discussion between Richard Hamilton, Toni del Renzio and Reyner Banham.

**28** D. Riesman, *The Lonely Crowd*, Yale University Press, New Haven, 1961, p. 46.

**29** R. Banham, 'The Machine Aesthetic', *Architectural Review*, 1955, p. 227.

**30** D. Riesman, *The Lonely Crowd*, p. 46.

**31** R. Banham, *Theory and Design in the First Machine Age*, Architectural Press, 1960, p. 9.

**32** A. C. Spectorsky, *The Exurbanites*, J. B. Lippincott & Co., Philadelphia & New York, 1955, pp. 7–8.

**33** *Ibid.*, p. 3.

**34** R. Banham, 'The Atavism of the Short-Distance Mini-Cyclist', *Living Arts*, No. 3, 1964, p. 92.

**35** J. McHale, *Fathers of Pop*, discussion between Mary and Reyner Banham, Magda Cordell and John McHale, pp. 29–30.

**36** R. Banham, 'Vehicles of Desire', *Art*, 1 September 1955, p. 3.

# 7

## *This is Tomorrow* and beyond

THE INDEPENDENT Group last met in July 1955. Whilst the historiography of the Independent Group emphasises the impact which it made on the succeeding generations of Pop artists, there is little evidence to substantiate this claim. Following the demise of the Group, the issues that had arisen at the meetings were incorporated into the writing and art work of the erstwhile members. The theory of the Expendable Aesthetic, the reworking of modernism and the cultural continuum were all evident in the work of the Independent Group during the later 1950s and the 1960s. However, it is arguable whether this led to the creation of Pop Art; by the time the so-called 'second and third generations'[1] of Pop artists had begun to make an impact the Independent Group had not existed for seven years. Where there is evidence of the young proto-Pop artists making contact with the Independent Group they appear to have already formulated their own approach to mass culture and modernism. What is fascinating is the way in which the Independent Group's closet discussions matured into powerful public statements in the later 1950s rather than speculation on their alleged influence upon artists. The most lasting impact which the Group made was on the thinking of younger critics and writers, particularly Roger Coleman. The Group's theories were new, challenging and exciting, which is what made the art so interesting. And it was this aspect of the Group's work which has had a far-reaching impact which remains largely unacknowleged.

According to Reyner Banham 'we ceased to exist in the spring of 1955, just stopped holding meetings and faded away. We had said and done what we wanted to say and do.'[2] The last mention of the Independent Group to appear in ICA records occurs on 17 March 1955 when Dorothy Morland reported that Gillo Dorfles was on a visit to London from Italy for the exhibition, *Italian Industrial Design* at the Italian Institute, and could talk to the Group. In terms of other written evidence, the last meeting took place on 15 July 1955 to hear Frank Cordell discuss 'Gold Pan Alley'.[3] The Group ceased to meet after this session, largely because it had fulfilled its purpose. The members of the Independent Group were no longer the marginalised young upstarts at the ICA. Lawrence Alloway was appointed Assistant Director of the Institute in July 1955, thus ensuring that he could wield more power within the ICA to organise exhibitions and lecture programmes.

Alloway organised a lecture series on Mass Communications during late 1955. When the series was announced in the *Bulletin* there were no claims to its being controversial or unrepresentative of the management's views, as had been the case with his 1954 series of talks on the cinema. The series of three talks under the heading 'Mass Communications' certainly reflected the concerns of the second session of the Independent Group. The talks aimed to interpret the new mass culture of post-war Britain in terms of the challenge which it presented to traditional aesthetics. The series began with Toni del Renzio talking on 'Fashion and Fashion Magazines' on 25 October 1955. This was a subject which had already been discussed at an earlier Independent Group meeting of 24 June. The second talk, also chaired by Lawrence Alloway, followed the earlier Independent Group pattern of inviting certain experts to lecture. In this case John Nicholson Low, editor of *The Dandy* for twenty years, Geoffrey Trease, the author of *Tales out of School* and G. Harry McLaughlin, who had formerly worked on a children's newspaper, met to discuss 'Children's Books and Periodicals'. The final session of the series was concerned with 'The Audience as Consumer: Independent Television and Audience Research' on 12 January 1956. Participants included: Dr H. W. Durant, the director of Social Surveys Limited, and Bernard Sendall, Deputy Director-General of the Independent Television Authority from 1955 to 1977 and author of the standard texts on the history of the organisation, *Independent Television in Britain* (Vol. I 1982 and vol. II 1983).

Other members of the Independent Group were now enjoying some measure of success beyond the ICA. Magda Cordell held a solo show at the Hanover Gallery in March 1956; Hamilton held his first solo show there in January 1955, and both Paolozzi and Henderson took part in the exhibition of contemporary sculpture there in July 1956. Paolozzi was now teaching sculpture at St Martin's School of Art and won the Copely Foundation Award in 1956. Reyner Banham resigned from the Managing Committee on 18 June 1956 to concentrate on his Ph.D thesis at the Courtauld Institute of Art and his work at the *Architectural Review*. Another contributing factor towards the cessation of the Independent Group was that various members no longer lived or worked in London. Nigel Henderson was living in an old smugglers' inn inherited from his in-laws at Thorpe-le-Soken. The Paolozzi family moved into the adjoining cottages in 1955 and Henderson and Paolozzi founded Hammer Prints Limited to produce textiles and ceramics. Richard Hamilton was teaching full-time in Newcastle, and John McHale left London in 1955 on a one-year Yale Fellowship. This was to study colour theory with Bauhaus master Josef Albers which rein-forced his rejection of modernism and stimulated his interest in American mass culture and communication theory.

The Group members still kept in touch with one another and such contact bore fruit. Alloway wrote the exhibition catalogue for Magda Cordell in 1956 and Reyner Banham wrote the definitive book on the Smithsons, *New Brutalism: Ethic or Aesthetic* (1966). Lawrence Alloway and Toni del Renzio worked together on the *Dimensions* exhibition of abstract painting at the O'Hara Gallery, London, in 1957. The show included five members of the Independent Group, calling into question once again the accepted account of the Group which explains its significance as the instiga-tor of Pop Art. Another example of the continuing collaboration of the Group is Alloway's account of Eduardo Paolozzi's early work, *Metallization of a Dream* (1963), which identifies the importance of Paolozzi's stay in Paris and the debt he owed to Max Ernst.

The most celebrated case of the Group's continuing collaboration was the exhibition, *This is Tomorrow* at the Whitechapel Art Gallery, staged between 9 August and 9 September 1956. This was one of the most popular shows of 1956 with 19,341 visitors, and 1,445 cata-logues sold. The catalogue itself was an important piece of graphic design by Edward Wright. Unusually for a gallery exhibition, it received widespread media coverage from Pathé Gazette, Pathé Pictorial, television and newspapers – both national and local. The Exhibition forms an important facet in the historiography of the Independent Group, in that it is often erroneously presumed that the Group was entirely responsible for the show. However, this was not the case; only twelve of the thirty-six participants were ex-Independent Group members. The idea to encourage collaboration between 'one architect, one painter and one sculptor,'[4] had been floated by architectural writer J. M. Richards in 1950. It was a prevalent area of concern at that time, particularly amongst the British Constructivists. A further impetus came from the French Groupe Espace whose London-based representative, Paule Vezelay, contacted Leslie Martin about the idea of holding a collaborative exhibition. Martin brought in his London County Council colleague, Colin St John Wilson to work on the concept. Stormy meetings followed between *Architectural Design*'s editor Theo Crosby, and Victor Pasmore, Robert Adams, Roger Hilton, Adrian Heath and Vezelay. According to Heath, Lawrence Alloway was also involved in the planning of the exhibition from an early stage.[5] This seems likely as Alloway contributed an introduction to the exhibition catalogue, in which he proposed that the results of the collaboration between architect, painter and sculptor in *This is Tomorrow* blew apart the theories of the modern movement.[6] Reyner Banham was also involved from the planning stages, approaching Bryan Robertson of the Whitechapel Gallery in March 1955 about staging the exhibition. He too contributed an introduction to the catalogue, again on the theme of the bankruptcy of modernism.

Whilst *This is Tomorrow* is frequently celebrated as the birthplace of Pop Art, the overarching concept was that of design. Subsequently neglected in chronicles of the Group, as fine art still occupies a place at the pinnacle of cultural achievement – design is located further down in the order of merit, despite the efforts of the Group itself. Alloway's introduction, entitled 'Design as Human Activity', describes the twelve stands as being 'designed' in deliberate contradiction to one other in an attempt to recreate the chaos of the street as opposed to the precious world of modernist rhetoric. Alloway concludes by claiming this is 'the biggest show about design and ways of life since the MARS group exhibition in 1937.'[7] Banham's introduction reinforces the importance of the design theory theme. Expressed in the form of free verse, he constructs a stimulating overview of modernist design theory from the Gesamtkunstwerk, the Bauhaus to Max Bill. The third introduction by Constructivist David Lewis differed from those of the two ex-Independent Group members in that he maintained that the tenets of modernism could be adapted to suit the needs of the 1950s and beyond.

This major difference among the three introductions summarises the divided nature of *This is Tomorrow*. Those seven groups of architects, sculptors and painters who contributed towards the exhibition and had not been involved with the Independent Group relied upon Constructivism for the solution to the problem of integrating art and design. Indeed, Group Five, which consisted of John Ernest, Anthony Hill and Denis Williams, designed its space to capture the spirit of the decade 1913 to 1923. The display of reproductions of work by Malevich and Gabo was included in this celebration of the 'heroic' years of Constructivism. The parts of the exhibition designed by those who had been involved with the Independent Group certainly reflected Group interests, but not only in the area of American mass culture, as is often presumed to be the case.

Toni del Renzio and Lawrence Alloway formed a group with John Holroyd who had made an important visit to America in 1953–54 where he met Charles and Ray Eames and saw *A Communication Primer*, to be shown later at the ICA. The Group's solution to the problem of integration of the arts was to treat all cultural processes as communication. Important research into the area of communication was then taking place at Yale. With the aid of simple diagrams, borrowed from American communications theory, they demonstrated that the narrow aesthetic definitions which divide painting and architecture can be overcome if both are regarded as communication (Figure 37). The Independent Group had discussed this concept in the meeting guested by E. W. Meyer. Alloway had sustained his interest in communications by proposing a lecture course for the ICA on *Aspects of Communication* which began in the spring of 1956 and included guest speakers who had been instrumental in establishing the Communications Research Centre at University College, London. Hence, J. F. Warburg, secretary of the Centre, spoke on 'Poetry and the Machine; Some Communicative Problems' and N. F. Dixon of the Psychology Department lectured on 'Information Theory and its Application to Psychology'.

Nigel Henderson, Eduardo Paolozzi and Peter and Alison Smithson, who had formed something of a clique within the Independent Group, continued to explore the concerns first raised in *Parallel of Life and Art* in 1953. The environment created in the patio and pavilion was one of crudeness, with rough-hewn rocks, sand, gravel and a very basic, shed-like structure (Figure 38). This section of *This is Tomorrow* referred to the Independent Group's concern with the implications of technology and the reading of symbolism. The space presented:

the fundamental necessities of the human habitat in a series of symbols. The first necessity is for a piece of the world – the patio. The second necessity is for an enclosed space – the pavilion. The two spaces are furnished with symbols for all human needs.[8]

The difference between this section and the supposedly proto-Pop environment created by Richard Hamilton, John Voelcker and John McHale is often stressed.[9] However, there are telling similarities in that both aimed to create a total, symbolic environment.

The environment created by Hamilton, Voelcker and McHale did not concentrate on the primitive, subconscious needs of men and women but on the problems of perception (Figure 40). Whilst the section did include examples of mass culture, for example the giant cut-out of Marilyn Monroe and Robbie the Robot – the latter borrowed from the opening of the film *The Forbidden Planet* – these were conceived of as forming part of the total environment. The space also incorporated soft floors, fluorescent paint dribbled on to surfaces and references to optical illusions (Figures 39 and 41). John McHale was in the United States on a Yale Fellowship for some of the time during which the exhibition was being prepared, and sent material back to Richard Hamilton which was used in the exhibition. For example, the discs which adorned one wall were enlargements of material given to John McHale on a visit to Marcel Duchamp.[10] As John McHale recalled, the overall aim of the exhibition design was to 'upset people's conventional orientation frameworks. Upset their perceptions . . . of space, time,'[11] and this was done with the creation of a fun house environment, which drew heavily on cultural symbolism for its effect.

Reyner Banham acknowledged similarities between the *Parallel of Life and Art* team's section and that of Hamilton, Voelcker and McHale:

37] Double page spread from the *This Is Tomorrow* exhibition catalogue featuring Geoffrey Holroyd, Toni del Renzio and Lawrence Alloway's section

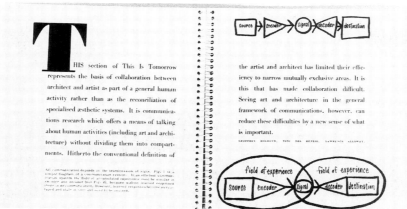

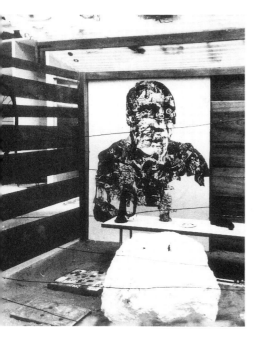

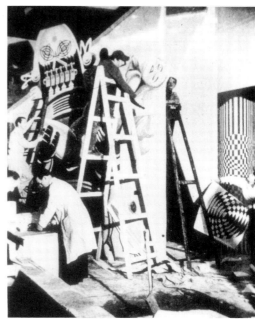

The *This is Tomorrow* exhibition (1956)

**38]** Alison and Peter Smithson, Nigel Henderson and Eduardo Paolozzi's 'Patio and Pavilion' section

**39]** Richard Hamilton, Terry Hamilton, John McHale and Magda Cordell erecting their section

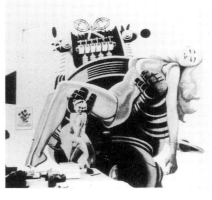

**40]** Section designed by Richard Hamilton, John McHale and John Voelcker featuring a cut-out Marilyn Monroe and Robbie the Robot from *The Forbidden Planet*

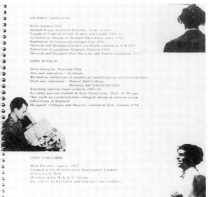

**41]** Double page spread from Richard Hamilton *et al.*'s contribution to the catalogue

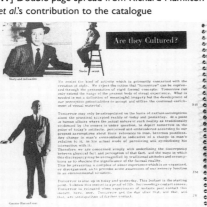

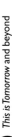

Yet, curiously, their section seemed to have more in common with that of the New Brutalists than any other, and the clue to this kinship would appear to lie in the fact that neither relied upon abstract concepts, but on concrete images – images that can carry the mass of tradition and association, or the energy of novelty and technology, but resist classification by the geometrical disciplines by which most other exhibits were dominated.[12]

Banham is reiterating the importance of the concept of 'Image' which he had introduced in his 1955 article on New Brutalism. The quote also refers to the Independent Group's reluctance to propose any absolute theory with which to evaluate visual culture. As Banham pointed out, the difference between the two Independent Group's exhibition designs and the remainder lay in their refusal to illustrate any abstract, aesthetic theory and their desire to create an environment using the most readily available materials. The images selected, whether from mass culture, science, technology or nature were thought to contain their own systems of signification and to shift according to individual spectator's knowledge and experience. The challenge was for the audience to extract his or her own meaning from the exhibits, without reference to abstract concepts. In a symposium, broadcast by the BBC, Richard Hamilton stressed: 'we have intended all the way through to hit as hard as we can to make the observer look more closely at everything'.[13] The reluctance to work with abstract concepts was criticised by Colin St John Wilson during the discussions:

Neither Smithson with his ludicrously antediluvian objects, nor Hamilton with his ludicrously streamlined pop art are in fact making a constructive statement at all. They are merely lumping together formless phenomena.[14]

The elevation of the pivotal role of the audience in the interpretation of meaning is vital to any understanding of consumer culture and provides an invaluable critical approach to one of the most significant phenomena in twentieth-century society. The Group's critique of modernism and the high/low culture divide was seminal as was the new understanding of consumption and audience. But, apart from *This is Tomorrow*, how were these ideas disseminated?

Because the Independent Group largely functioned as a testing ground for new ideas, the content of its meetings did not become public knowledge until the later 1950s through the broadcast and print media and ICA events. There were rarely more than twenty people at any one Independent Group meeting and the nature of the discussions was not reflected in the work of its members at the time. Banham was contributing articles to the *Architectural Review* on the history of modern architecture, Alloway was writing criticism for *Art News*, and Hamilton was exhibiting the *Trainsition* paintings at the Hanover Gallery. The Independent Group made little impact during its lifespan, it was only after the demise of the Group in July 1955 that the fruits of its discussions began to reach a wider audience, firstly at the ICA.

In July 1955 Alloway was appointed Assistant Director of the Institute and more time was devoted to discussing the problems which mass culture raised for the fine arts. The Independent Group no longer met clandestinely, but talks which had been given at its meetings now formed part of the public programme. Toni del Renzio had spoken on *Fashion and Fashion Magazines* to the Group in June 1955. He repeated his lecture before an audience of ICA members on 25 October of the same year; it was also published by the Institute in 1956 in pamphlet form. *After a fashion* as it was titled, applied Independent Group preoccupations with expendability and symbolism to the fashion industry. This theme was explored further in 1957 when he applied Dr S. Vaijda's theory of games to an understanding of *The Strategies of Fashion*. Banham also contributed to the ICA's programme in the later 1950s on themes arising from Independent Group meetings. In December 1957 he lectured on the apparent conflict between traditional taste and mass culture. In the précis of *The Trapeze and the Human Pyramid* he used 'pop' in its original sense of meaning mass culture and examined the 'competition between "top" and "Pop", and . . . some of the social consequences of skilled aesthetic technicians (musicians, graphic designers, writers etc.) being able to choose between two masters, instead of being at the mercy of Establishment taste.'[15] Hamilton also brought Independent Group concerns to a wider audience in 1959 with his lecture on *The Design Image of the 50s*, which was later published in *Design* magazine as 'Persuading Image'.[16]

The results of Independent Group discussions often became better known through publication of edited versions in magazines. Former members continued to pursue the issues which had surfaced during the meetings and had remained unresolved. Banham wrote about the bankruptcy of modernism and the need to come to terms with the full implications of mass production, in a comprehensive set of articles throughout the 1950s and 1960s.[17] The Smithsons attempted to formulate an architecture within the terms of the Expendable Aesthetic in their *House of the Future*, designed for the Ideal Home Exhibition in March 1956 (Figure 42). This was a fantasy home designed for the year 1981 to be moulded from 'plastic impregnated fibrous plaster.'[18] Planned around a central core of

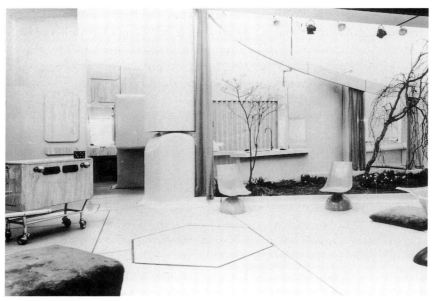

**42]** Alison and Peter Smithson, *House of the Future* (1956)

services, the rooms contained the latest gadgets, including a micro-wave cooker and aluminium, disposable containers. The house stimulated immense public interest and was featured on newsreels, complete with space-age inhabitants, and described in the *Newnes Homebook of Household Management*. John McHale, in an article commissioned by Gillo Dorfles for the book *Kitsch* in 1968, was still debating notions of expendability and the continuum of culture.[19]

This underlines both the importance of the issues raised by the Independent Group, and their open-endedness. As Lawrence Alloway commented in 1977 'One of the things in retrospect that makes me think highly of the Independent Group is the extent to which the ideas were developable.'[20]

### The next generation

Existing histories of the Independent Group stress the continuity between the Group and the subsequent generations of Pop paint-ers. However, a fresh look at the evidence does not substantiate this claim. It seems that those painters involved in the creation of Pop Art in the 1960s regarded the Independent Group as a rather insular clique, whose work was little known. David Hockney recalled that Richard Hamilton was 'actually teaching in the College, in the School of Interior Design. Nobody knew of his work much. We knew it later, but not then.'[21] Richard Smith, in an interview with Reyner Banham, recalled that his first contact with the Independent Group was at the opening of Madga Cordell's exhibition of *Monotypes and Collages* which took place in the ICA Library in July 1955. By this time the Independent Group had ceased to meet. Richard Smith, when asked to define the influence of the Independent Group on his own generation responded candidly: 'I can't see it specifically. I mean, I must say that I didn't like the art. I think the painting of my generation took off from other sources'.[22] Perhaps, by the late 1950s, mass culture was an all-pervading aspect of life, and could not be ignored. The Pop artists who made such an impact in the early 1960s would have included references to mass culture in their work, whether the Independent Group had existed or not. The strenuous attempts on behalf of subsequent historians to establish a respectable heritage for 1960s Pop Art reveal the narrative emphasis of traditional art history.

It is certainly true that there were some concrete links between the ex-members of the Independent Group and the Royal College of Art through Roger Coleman – however, these were more in terms of theory and approach than artistic influence. Coleman was the editor of *Ark*, the College student magazine, during 1957 and he formed a close relationship with Alloway at this time. Alloway contributed towards two editions of *Ark* along with other members of the Group.[23] Roger Coleman also began to play a part at the ICA during 1957. In February he took part in a dialogue with Richard Smith on *Man about Mid-Century*, in which they discussed trends in menswear in the 1950s. Coleman also became a member of the Exhibitions Sub-Committee in March 1957, joining Theo Crosby, Robert Melville, Roland Penrose, Toni del Renzio and Lawrence Alloway. Smith was given the opportunity to exhibit at the ICA in *Five Young Painters* during January 1958 and *Place* with Robyn Denny and Ralph Rumney in September 1959. Whilst their work was not the fully fledged Pop Art of the 1960s, it did include references to mass culture. Coleman was at pains to point out that these artists 'regard "Astounding Science Fiction" as more essential reading than, say, Roger Fry.'[24] Coleman used Independent Group material again in his introduction to *Place*, when he explained 'The mass media for Denny, Rumney and Smith is not a source of imagery, but a source of ideas that act as stimuli and as orientation in a cultural continuum.'[25]

This echoed the Group's view that culture should be classified along a horizontal axis rather than a traditional vertical hierarchy. Coleman makes an important distinction here between the incorporation of popular imagery into painting and the wider connotations of the pop sensibility. It was the ideas generated by the ICA discussions which stimulated artists like Hamilton, Paolozzi and Smith. The later manifestations of the Pop Art movement should be regarded as a separate entity rather than the fulfilment of the work begun in the 1950s. The Group's critique of modernist design theory and their elevation of popular taste and the stylist were also reflected in Coleman's writing, notably 'Will Success spoil Industrial Design?' in *Architecture and Building* (August 1959).

Discussion on mass culture at the ICA culminated in 1961 with a series of talks organised by Robert Freeman. *Image of Tomorrow* brought erstwhile Independent Group members and younger artists together for the last time. Alloway explored the iconology of science fiction and McHale summarised much of the Group thinking on culture in *The Plastic Parthenon*, published in *Cambridge Opinion* in 1960. The obvious curtailment of material on the whole question of redefining culture could be linked with Alloway's resignation from the ICA staff in September 1960 to be appointed Curator of the Guggenheim Museum, New York in July 1961. Relations between himself and Herbert Read had been perpetually strained, and a letter from Read to Penrose on 24 June 1959 reveals the general dissatisfaction of the ICA management with his performance:

Lawrence has committed another serious gaffe, this time with Colla. It has needed all Dorothy's (Morland) diplomacy to soothe him. The Lawrence problem is getting serious and Dorothy (who used to be so faithful to him) is now very worried. He is completely unreliable (in the administrative sense); he is doing practically no work for the £500 a year he receives from us; he alienates a considerable number of our potential friends; and I doubt if he is loyal. I also understand that he receives fees (probably from Power) for buying and selling which I consider absolutely défendu for a member of our staff.[26]

Alloway had remained convinced of the need to come to terms with new manifestations of mass culture throughout the 1950s, and this conviction had led to the promulgation of pop sensibility at the ICA, probably to the dismay of Read who described Pop Art as 'tedious' in a letter to Roland Penrose.[27] Younger artists no longer regarded mass culture with disdain. The 'second generation' of pop painters had definitely benefited from the breadth of the Institute's programme in a general sense. By 1962 the term Pop Art had attracted a much narrower definition and referred instead to a particular style in art. Instead of defending their broader use of the term, Alloway and Banham attempted to carve a niche for the

Independent Group in the Pop Art lineage, the process of which is detailed in the next chapter. This was to belittle the achievements of the Group and recast it in an inappropriate mould. Pop Art took images from mass culture and incorporated them into painting and sculpture. The Independent Group succeeded in avoiding the elitism of other cultural theorists and arrived at a highly productive critical framework for the understanding of all aspects of visual culture. This is an approach which remains as fruitful and stimulating today as it was in the 1950s but is still unrecognised with some notable exceptions.

## Notes

1 See, for example, L. Alloway, 'The Development of British Pop' in L. Lippard, *Pop Art*, Thames & Hudson, 1978, p. 200.

2 R. Banham, *Fathers of Pop*, revised draft script, p. 7.

3 Notes on the Independent Group Session of 1955, unpublished MS, Alison and Peter Smithson Archives. See Appendix 2.

4 J. M. Richards, Transcription of a discussion on 'The Functions and Aims of an Institute of Contemporary Arts' held 18 April 1950 at the Architectural Association, p. 5. ICA Archives.

5 Adrian Heath in interview with author, 7 January 1984.

6 An extract from Alloway's introduction was printed in *Architectural Design*, September 1956.

7 *This is Tomorrow* exhibition catalogue, unpaginated.

8 *Ibid*.

9 *Ibid*.

10 *Fathers of Pop*, discussion between John McHale, Magda Cordell, Mary and Reyner Banham, p. 39 of transcript.

11 *Ibid*.

12 R. Banham, 'This is Tomorrow', *Architectural Review*, September 1956, p. 188.

13 Transcript of a symposium attended by Peter Smithson, Colin St John Wilson, William Turnbull, Richard Hamilton, Anthony Hill, Theo Crosby and David Piper. Broadcast on the Third Programme on 17 August 1956, p. 3. Tate Gallery Archives.

14 *Ibid*.

15 ICA *Bulletin*, December 1957, p. 3.

16 R. Hamilton, 'Persuading Image', *Design*, February 1960, pp. 28–32.

17 See for example, R. Banham, 'Design By Choice' in *Architectural Review*, July 1961 and 'The Great Gizmo' in *Industrial Design*, September 1965, both reprinted in P. Sparke (ed.), *Design By Choice*, Academy Editions, 1981.

18 A. & P. Smithson, 'House of the Future at the Ideal Home Exhibition', *Architectural Design*, March 1956, p. 101.

19 J. McHale, 'The Plastic Parthenon' in G. Dorfles, *Kitsch*, first published in Italian by Gabriele Mazzottax, Milan, 1968. First published in English by Studio Vista, 1969, pp. 98–110.

**20** L. Alloway, in interview with Reyner Banham for *Fathers of Pop*, 25 May 1977, p. 2.

**21** D. Hockney, *David Hockney*, Thames & Hudson, 1976, p. 42.

**22** R. Smith, in interview with Reyner Banham for *Fathers of Pop*, p. 2.

**23** *Ark* No. 17, summer 1956, 'Technology and Sex in Science Fiction: A Note on Cover Art'; No. 20, autumn 1957, 'Communication Comedy and the Small World' by Lawrence Alloway. Alison and Peter Smithson's essay 'But Today We Collect Ads' in issue 18. Frank Cordell wrote an article on his profession entitled 'Gold Pan Alley' and John McHale 'Technology and the Home' in issue 20, autumn 1957. Toni del Renzio's 'Shoes, Hair and Coffee' also appeared in this issue.

**24** R. Coleman, Introduction to *Five Young Painters* exhibition catalogue, ICA, 1958.

**25** R. Coleman, *Guide to Place*, exhibition catalogue, ICA, 1959.

**26** H. Read, Unpublished MS, letter to Roland Penrose, 24 June 1959. Penrose Archives.

**27** H. Read, Unpublished MS, letter to Roland Penrose, 28 February 1960. Penrose Archives.

# The myth of the Independent Group: historiography and hagiology

THE ACCEPTED history of the Independent Group is tanta-mount to a myth. Existing accounts range from the inaccurate to the overtly untrue. All the published material on the Independent Group relies on and reinforces an unquestioned ret-rospective account, indicated by the term, the myth of the Independent Group. Initially, it is essential to chronicle how the Group emerged as a historical phenomenon, to be included in every history of Pop Art and history of post-war British culture. Although the Group met from 1952 to 1955, the first published reference to it did not appear in England until 1960.[1] Even unpub-lished mentions of the Independent Group in ICA correspondence and minutes are scant. The myth of the Independent Group is based largely upon articles by former Group members published in the early 1960s. These articles came as a direct response to a specif-ic historical situation and their validity as a source material needs to be questioned.

The two most prolific writers within the Independent Group, Reyner Banham and Lawrence Alloway, never mentioned it by name during its existence in spite of the fact that, for example, Banham was a regular contributor to *Encounter, Art News and Review, Art* and *Architectural Review* (frequently on subjects which would have interested, and probably grew out of discussions with, the Group). Similarly, Alloway's reviews and articles which appeared in *Art News and Review* on a regular basis never once hinted at the exis-tence of the Independent Group. Fresh evidence indicates that the Independent Group, in the words of Dorothy Morland, 'Could not have been less formal'.[2] This partly explains why the myth has arisen. The Group was such a relaxed, informal and small affair that no 'official' documentation, such as minutes, ever existed. Hence, it probably never occurred to Alloway or Banham at the time that discussions taking place amongst their circle were particularly significant. Also, because of this informality, it is difficult to document the actual events and define the nature of the Group accurately. This could explain why the Independent Group has been misrepresented in current histories, as the sole starting point for such an account has been the former members themselves, whether it be their published writing or unpublished reminiscences. The Group has become an empty sign on to which any preoccupation or enthusiasm can be projected.

The phenomenon of the Independent Group was first brought to the attention of a wide public during a fifteen-part series of discussions on the Third Programme. In his introduction to the series, *Art-Anti-Art*, on 2 November, 1959, Basil Taylor identified a concurrent thread in twentieth-century art to that of the modern movement. According to Taylor, this Anti-Art lineage began with Futurism, moved through l'art brut and art autre and concluded with *This is Tomorrow*. The sixth talk in the series, 'Primitives of a Mechanised Art' of 21 November 1959, consisted of Banham eulogising the Futurists. He referred to the images of popular culture so beloved by the Futurists: 'These images describe the London scene into which we stepped as we left the Institute of Contemporary Art those evenings in 1953 and 1954'.[3]

However, it was not until the final discussion of the series, 'Artists as Consumers: The Splendid Bargain', broadcast on 11 March 1960 that the Independent Group was mentioned by name. Participating in the debate over the role of the artist in society with reference to popular culture (or pop art as it was referred to then) were Richard Hamilton, Eduardo Paolozzi, Lawrence Alloway and Basil Taylor. Hamilton recalled:

I think the change in my attitude came in meeting a group of people who were concerned about something very dear to them. This was a thing called the Independent Group at the ICA. I think most art movements came out of a group of people who were beginning to concern themselves with such problems as why do we go to the cinema three times a week in 1952? why do we all buy *Life* magazine, when we can afford to buy *Esquire?* and all these questions began to assume great importance for us, and a period of analysis took place of these motives and I found it very valuable.

Although edited out in the broadcast, Alloway's response is recorded in the original script:

Well I remember those Independent Group meetings with tremendous affection and interest. I think one of the things that happened at these meetings, although I don't know that we realised it at the time . . . is that a different attitude towards leisure was emerging.

Paolozzi assessed the relevance of the Group slightly differently:

The whole thing about this . . . the Independent Group and the cinema and cutting pictures out of magazines, the important thing is the kind of redefinition of a new kind of person. We can forget about art for the moment.[4]

It was not until the impact of Pop Art in 1962 that the Independent Group ceased to be remembered as an informal discussion group.

The Independent Group was first mentioned in an English publication in February 1960, in a review of the Cambridge Group entitled 'Notes on Abstract Art and the Mass Media', which appeared in *Art News and Review*. The reference appeared in a footnote thus:

It is noticeable that no significant differences have yet emerged in the definition of pop art's role in the environment. TIT *Ark* and 'Talk' rest on the original unrevised hunches and research of the IG.[5]

The reason for the inclusion of the Independent Group in a footnote appeared six years later: 'This footnote was never intended for public enlightenment . . . it was more like a code message to forty or fifty readers.'[6] Therefore, Alloway did not grant the Group the historical prestige it was later to acquire but presented it as being a clique of close acquaintances. The footnote does encapsulate the notion that was to provide the basis for Alloway's subsequent writing on Pop Art and the Independent Group. The basic assumption which Alloway made is that the Independent Group had been the instigator of a new aesthetic, which encompassed fine art and 'pop art'. It is crucial that Alloway's meaning of 'pop art' is distinguished from later usages of the term. By 'pop art' Alloway meant technologically reproduced, visual popular culture:

The connection between fine and pop art, then, is not basically one of subject matter. Neither is it a short cut to being hip. The difference the arrival of pop art makes to art is part of a larger shift in attitude. As a result of psychological, sociological and historical study, and a sensitivity to iconology, art can now be sited within a general field of visual communication.[7]

The Group was not alone in its use of the term 'pop art'. For example, the publisher's 'blurb' on the back of Tom Harrison's book *Britain Revisited* (1961) also refers to the same phenomenon in terms of the mass media. The description of the genesis of a new aesthetic formed a major component of Alloway's writing of the late 1950s. 'Technology and Sex in Science Fiction', which appeared in *Ark* during 1956, 'The Arts and the Mass Media' of 1958 and 'The Long Front of Culture' of 1959 all pursue the theme of a non-hierarchical analysis of culture. However, it was not until 1960 that Alloway equated this view of culture with the 'IG'[8] and only in 1962 did he incorporate it into his formulation of the 'three generations', and adopt the conventional meaning of Pop Art as painting. Alloway's major contribution to the myth has been the proposition that British Pop Art developed in three distinct stages or generations, the Independent Group constituting the first phase. Alloway first explored this theme in the seminal article 'Pop Art since 1949' which appeared in the *Listener* (27 December 1962) and was broadcast on 8 December 1962 on the Third Programme. In this article, Alloway identified Francis Bacon as a precedent of Pop Art as Bacon relied upon popular imagery as a source for his paintings between 1949 and 1951. This was an opinion which has been expressed by Robert Melville during an ICA 'Points of View' lecture on 'Bacon and Balthus' which took place on 15 January 1952. Melville had compared Bacon's screaming popes with certain images in *Battleship Potemkin* during the discussion, which Alloway as a member of the ICA would almost certainly have attended.[9]

Alloway establishes Bacon as a precedent of Pop Art, but identifies the Independent Group as the main instigator. However, whilst Alloway mentions the principal Group members and refers to *Parallel of Life and Art* and *Man, Machine and Motion*, he never uses the title, Independent Group. Perhaps, even by this stage, Alloway thought of the Group as a nebulous gathering of friends with common interests rather than a distinct historical entity. This was not the case four years later when Alloway's chapter on British Pop formed part of Lucy Lippard's anthology, *Pop Art* (1966). This essay again located the importance of the Independent Group within the three-generation criterion, but for the first time Alloway actually refers at length to it by name. This could possibly be explained by the distance, both temporal and geographical, which Alloway had undergone by this stage in his career.[10] However, it could also be explained by Banham's contemporary writing on the same subject. Banham found Alloway's account in *Pop Art* to be accurate, if not a little academic:

We younger members of the Independent Group used to rather laugh up our sleeves at him, at the way he kept all the exhibition catalogues and filed all the newspaper cuttings and made himself the keeper of the bibliography, as we said.

During the same review, Banham could not resist including his own interpretation of events, summarised as 'I think we were having a belated teenage revolt'.[11]

Other reviewers were perhaps less eager to accept totally Alloway's history of British Pop. Robert Melville, who was involved with the ICA during the time of the Independent Group and chaired the Aesthetics of Modern Art series, wrote of the book 'All the contributors to Pop Art have a lot to say about their favourite "precursors". The book includes a well illustrated essay on English Pop by Lawrence Alloway, which rather too obviously underplays the importance of Peter Blake'.[12]

Despite Melville's objections, Alloway's contribution to *Pop Art* has become a standard text. *Pop Art* was published as one of the respectable World of Art series, simultaneously with five other titles including Edward Fry's *Cubism* and Michael Levey's *Rococo to Revolution*. Reyner Banham was the first to write in any length on the Independent Group, although not in such respectable publications as Alloway. Almost simultaneous with the appearance of Alloway's first treatise on Pop painting came Banham's first published reference to the Group 'Who is this Pop?', in the winter 1962–63 edition of *Motif*. Presumably the impetus for both Banham and Alloway's articles of 1962 came from the impact made in London by the *Young Contemporaries* exhibitions at the RBA Galleries in 1961 and 1962[13] and Ken Russell's *Pop Goes the Easel* screened by the BBC on 25 March 1962 in the Monitor series.

The film, produced by Huw Wheldon, treated the four artists included rather like pop stars. The camera team supposedly spent an ordinary Saturday with Peter Blake, Derek Boshier, Peter Phillips and Pauline Boty. The total lifestyle of the Pop artist was deemed to be of interest. The film revealed the artists in bed, on pin tables, driving large American cars, painting at the Royal College of Art and partying at Richard Smith's Clerkenwell residence. Audience research recorded a rather negative response to the programme: 'a large proportion of the sample audience deplored this investigation into what they supposed is the beatnik level of the world of art'.[14] Former Independent Group members must have been galled by this representation of the Pop artist, as no credit for the initiation of such behaviour or attitudes was given to the Independent Group.

One of the major aims of both 'Pop Art Since 1949' and 'Who is this Pop?' is to draw attention to the Independent Group as the unacknowledged creators of Pop Art. Banham labelled them 'Pop's Fine-Art Egg-Heads' and claimed:

IG, the boys in question, were the Independent Group at the ICA whose activities around 1953–55 are at the bottom of all conscious Pop-Art activities in Fine-Art circles. The basic vocabulary, including the words Pop-Art themselves (analogy with Pop music), came into circulation via the IG, even if they weren't invented by them.[15]

Alloway was less explicit, but equally anxious to carve a niche in the history of Pop Art for the Independent Group:

Pop artists of the third and current phase deny this historical setting by the use they make of pop art elements. The effect of the first and second phases of pop was (and this was badly needed in the 'fifties') to reduce the idealism and snobbery of English aesthetics and art criticism. Now, however, happy in the playground of the opened-out situation, pop artists lack a grasp of the history their art belongs to, as well as a sense of the internal rigour necessary to art.[16]

Whilst Alloway always considers that the Independent Group undertook some sort of internal putsch in the art world, he has always rejected the notion of Pop painting embodying any overt political significance. In 1966 he wrote: 'The pleasurable filling of a role in urban life (instead of protesting or looking for more favourable circumstances) separated London artists both from the working-class bias of Richard Hoggart and from the angry young men'.[17]

The major difference between Alloway and Banham's accounts of the Independent Group lies in their assessments of its political impact. Banham's writings from the mid-1950s do not refer to the Independent Group by name. He does, however, allude to the existence of a small group of young, avant-garde architects and artists which he dubbed the 'New Brutalists'. Banham introduced the term in 1955:

Non-architecturally it describes the art of Dubuffet, some aspects of Jackson Pollock and of Appel, and the burlap painting of Alberto Burri – among foreign artists – and, say, Magda Cordell or Eduardo Paolozzi and Nigel Henderson among English artists. With these last two, the Smithsons collected and hung the ICA exhibition, *Parallel of Life and Art*, which, though it probably preceded the coining of the phase, is nevertheless regarded as a locus classicus of the movement.[18]

Banham has always been eager to invent and foster new terminology with journalistic élan. This may explain why he was the first to give an account of the Independent Group as well as of the New Brutalists. Whenever Banham discusses this collection of Independent Group members, he does so within the terms of a young generation challenging established opinion. This challenge involved the New Brutalists knowing more of the modern movement than their British elders in architectural school or practice. After becoming familiar with the concepts of modernism, the Brutalists attempted to supersede Le Corbusier *et al.*, hence, staying 'two steps ahead' of their elders. Banham launched New Brutalism in an article of that name in December 1955, in which he described its effect upon:

The mass of moderate architects, *hommes moyens sensuels*, have found their accepted practices for waiving the requirements of the conscience-code suddenly called into question; they have been put rudely on the spot.[19]

Banham identified the same tendency when reviewing Richard Hamilton's solo show at the Hanover in January 1955:

But with end of the war, when the simulacrum of the Modern Movement in Art which had been built up by the professional apologists of the School of Paris and of the English Romantic Revival was exposed as a bug-ridden, clapped-out, creaking-jointed old lay-figure, and a younger generation has to find out for themselves what really made that movement tick.[20]

The notion that the Independent Group embodied a class-based challenge to the bourgeois attitudes of the time was first expounded in Banham's 1964 article, 'The Atavism of the Short-Distance Mini-Cyclist'. Obviously construed as a response to *The Loneliness of the Long Distance Runner*, first published in 1958, Banham attempts to relate the Independent Group to the contemporary interest in working-class, popular culture which had surfaced in literature and film in Britain. Banham described himself as a 'scholarship boy' and proclaimed, 'The working class is where I come from'.[21] According to Banham, the common experience of American popular culture during the 'thirties' provided the basis for Independent Group activities: 'This was our scene. And I think this is true for a great many of us, especially those who made up the Independent Group, who were the pacemakers of the early and middle fifties in London'.[22]

Whilst Alloway was never to refer directly to the Independent Group again in published work of the 1960s, despite a lengthy article on 'Popular Culture and Pop Art' appearing in *Studio International*, July/August 1969, Banham frequently mentions the Group. The book *New Brutalism – ethic or aesthetic?* published in 1966 gives an account of the Group, again couched in terms of its rebellion against the establishment.[23] A sign that Banham's account of the Independent Group had received academic approval came with the inclusion of his paper, 'Detroit Tin Re-Visited' in the

1975 Conference, *Design: 1900–1960* held at Newcastle upon Tyne Polytechnic by the Division of History of Art and Complementary Studies. Later published as *Design 1900–1960 – Studies in Design and Popular Culture*, the volume includes Banham's essay which reworks certain familiar themes. On the subject of American car styling in the 1950s, Banham commented: 'Yet it seemed that only us members of the Independent Group at the ICA with our backs against the wall in Dover Street, had been given the gift to see it.'[24]

Banham's version of the history of the Independent Group reached new levels of respectability with the production of an Arts Council film in 1979. Entitled *The Fathers of Pop*, the film consists of a reiteration and reinforcement of the myth of the Independent Group, which Alloway and Banham have been responsible for creating. The role of the ICA is barely mentioned; existing institutions (such as the Courtauld Institute of Art) are assessed in negative terms; culture and technology are deemed to be the only areas of interest which gave rise to the Independent Group. The members of the Group are described as 'a rough lot' by Banham. Alloway's notion of the new aesthetic of culture is reiterated and attempts are made to demonstrate the impact of the Group on ensuing generations with little success. Whilst Banham admitted during the film that many myths have grown up about the Independent Group, he never questions them. Hence, the two views of the Group promulgated by Banham and Alloway are perfectly viable as personal reminiscences of events, but should not be accepted as historical fact at face value. However, this is what has tended to happen, as no other sources have been apparent for cultural historians wishing to include the Independent Group in their work.

## The assimilation of the myth of the Independent Group

By early 1963 the Independent Group was established within the history of art as the instigator of British Pop Art. The sources for any study of the Independent Group to date had been restricted to the often conflicting, retrospective accounts of Lawrence Alloway and Reyner Banham. Subsequent histories of Pop always include a résumé of Independent Group activities, either within the terms of Alloway's notion of the three generations of Pop artists, or of Banham's theory that the Independent Group instigated a working-class revolt.

Jasia Reichardt was the first non-Independent Group member to publish an account of it in the February 1963 issue of *Art International*.[25] Although Reichardt was not to join the staff of the

ICA until the following year, she was active there and information included in the article probably came from Richard Hamilton, Reyner Banham and Dorothy Morland. Obvious affinities between 'Pop Art and After', and 'Pop Art Since 1949' exist, particularly in the attempt to demonstrate the influence of the Independent Group on the 1962 generation of Pop artists. Two pieces of evidence are cited in 'Pop Art and After' to prove the influence of the Independent Group. The first is Richard Hamilton's collage, *Just What Is It That Makes Today's Homes So Different, So Appealing?* (1956) which Reichardt claimed to be 'The first piece of work in the pop art idiom . . . shown in 1956 at the Whitechapel Art Gallery in London in an exhibition called *This is Tomorrow*.'[26]

This claim has remained largely unchallenged by art historians. However, *Just What Is It . . .?* (1956) was not exhibited at *This is Tomorrow* as a work of art, because it was never originally intended as such. The collage was reproduced in black and white as a poster for the exhibition and printed in the catalogue. It is only in the light of subsequent developments in Pop that the collage reproduced on the cover of this book, has acquired a totally different meaning and has come to be regarded as a fine art object in itself (Figure 43).

Reichardt then set an influential precedent by following a discussion of *Just What Is It . . .?* with a quotation taken from a letter allegedly written by Richard Hamilton and sent to the Smithsons, dated 16 January 1957. The quotation reads:

> Pop Art is:
> Popular (designed for a mass audience)
> Transient (short term solutions)
> Expendable (easily forgettable)
> Low Cost
> Mass Produced
> Young (aimed at Youth)
> Witty
> Sexy
> Gimmicky
> Glamorous
> Big Business[27]

This quotation has come to be included in every history of Pop Art.

However, the entire letter was reprinted in Richard Hamilton's *Collected Words* (1982), and an analysis of the complete text puts an entirely new emphasis on the frequently quoted list of attributes of Pop Art. Hamilton was actually discussing the possibility of staging a follow-up exhibition to *This is Tomorrow* in his letter. It is worth quoting the letter in greater detail than is usual:

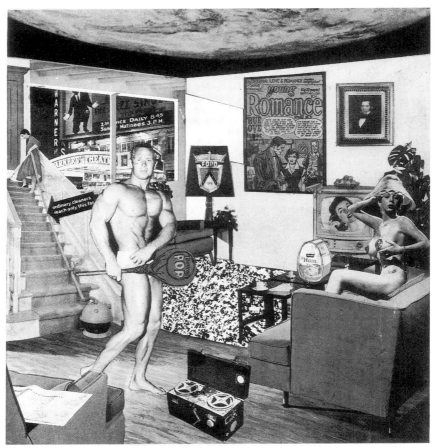

**43]** Richard Hamilton, 'Just What Is It That Makes Today's Homes So Different, So Appealing?', as it appeared in the *This is Tomorrow* exhibition catalogue. A collage drawn from American mass media sources, mainly supplied by John McHale as a result of his visit to Yale

The disadvantage (as well as the great virtue) of the TIT show was its incoherence and the absurdity of language. My view is that another show should be as highly disciplined and unified in conception as that one was chaotic.

Suppose we were to start with the objective of providing a unique solution to the specific requirements of a domestic environment e.g. some kind of covering, some kind of equipment, some kind of Art. This solution to be formulated and rated on the the basis of compliance with a table of characteristics of Pop Art.[28]

The familiar definition of Pop Art then follows this statement. It is crucial to realise that, like Lawrence Alloway before him, Hamilton meant visual mass culture by the term Pop Art, and not painting. However, the list of the attributes of Pop Art is often quoted erroneously with reference to painting.

Whilst Jasia Reichardt collected her source material for 'Pop Art and After' from past members of the Independent Group, a more intimate knowledge of the Group is demonstrated in David Sylvester's *Sunday Times Colour Supplement* article 'Art in a Coke Climate'. Sylvester's opening paragraph could have been penned by Alloway:

The point is not whether Coca-Cola culture is wiser and nicer than wine culture; the point is that it is a culture – a set of tribal tastes and customs which implies certain values and customs which implies certain attitudes and a conception of what life could ideally be.[29]

Sylvester also conducted a semiological comparison between an American car and a Rolls-Royce in support of an expendable aesthetic of industrial design. In the section entitled *When the Parthenon goes for a ride* Sylvester's debt to Banham's early writing on this subject cannot be ignored.[30] The first full-length book to be published in London on the subject of Pop Art was Mario Amaya's *Pop as Art: A Survey of the New Super-Realism*, which appeared in 1965. Amaya drew from both Reichardt and Alloway's articles, although there is no evidence of a reading of Banham. This is frequently the case with the histories of Pop Art written prior to the ascendancy of Marxist theory amongst academics during the late 1970s. Alloway's account has become common currency in standard art and design histories, possibly because of his diffidence on the issue of class which features so prominently in Banham's. Hence it is Alloway's version of events which informs standard works such as *The Oxford Companion to Art*,[31] *The Penguin Dictionary of Art and Artists*[32] and *Movements in Art since 1945*.[33] Also, what is perhaps the most extensive and informative account of British Pop Art to be published, *Pop Art Redefined*, reprints articles by Alloway and McHale[34] but neglected to include Banham.

Retrospective exhibitions of Group members Hamilton and Paolozzi held at the Tate, in 1970 and 1971 respectively, also relied heavily upon Alloway's version of the history of the Independent Group in their catalogues. Both artists' work is assessed within the canons of Pop Art. However, a new phenomenon in the assimilation of the myth now emerges. Frank Whitford (in his chapter 'Paolozzi and the Independent Group') accepts the myth without question but also includes new material in support of it. The new material could only have come from the recollections of the members themselves and, judging from inclusions in the article, Whitford had spoken to Banham and, of course, Paolozzi. For the first time Richard Lannoy is mentioned as the initial convenor of the Group and a more detailed description of Group meetings and public semi-nar programmes is included. Because the chapter is probably based mainly upon reminiscences of Paolozzi, his position within the myth tends to escalate. Instead of occupying his former role as an artist/member of the Group, Whitford attempted to establish him as a precursor of Independent Group ideas. Whitford's premise for such a claim is the *Bunk* series of collages (Figure 44), which he pro-posed constituted the first Independent Group meeting:

Such ideas were cultural heresy then, and in some quarters still are now, although an increasing acceptance of such notions is a mark of Paolozzi's and the Independent Group's influence. It took some time, however, before the Independent Group itself could fully accept the ideas implied by Paolozzi's first epidiascope. Once again, later writers have tended to trace the history of a concern with popular art in terms of all the Independent Group meetings, and especially through the paintings of Richard Hamilton. It is worth remembering that the only people collecting pulp imagery in the early 1950s were Francis Bacon and Paolozzi, and Hamilton, who derived his imagery for paintings like *Hers in a Lush Situation* (*sic*) (1957) directly from the slides Banham showed during his talk on automobile styling was, even in 1954, still interested in fine paint-ing related to Cézanne – see, for example, *Trainsition III* (1954). When the IG broke up Alloway was still convinced by Abstract Expressionism.[35]

Other ex-members of the Group have not been so eager to enhance their reputations by means of the myth. Nigel Henderson, in the catalogue of his first retrospective at Anthony d'Offay gallery during 1977, summed up his relation to the Group in interview thus:

Involved with the beginning of the Independent Group at the ICA. Recalls voting in Reyner Banham and Toni del Renzio. Attended Paolozzi's famous lecture at the first meeting of the IG and participated in several discussions there on his own account during the fifties. But for Henderson the ideas behind the IG were not so new and exciting. He already had his own contacts with scientists, and was older than most of the other members (Alloway, Hamilton, McHale, Turnbull *et al.*).[36]

Richard Hamilton showed no hesitation in acknowledging the importance of the Independent Group, but tended to question its representation in history:

Commuting weekly from and to London together with long university vacations, enabled me to retain contact with my friends in London, in par-ticular with the members, if that loose association of unlike spirits can be said to be a membership, of the Independent Group.[37]

Toni del Renzio is equally doubtful about the accuracy of the myth in his 1976 essay, 'Pop'. Del Renzio refers to the 'Hagiography' of the Independent Group, and warned:

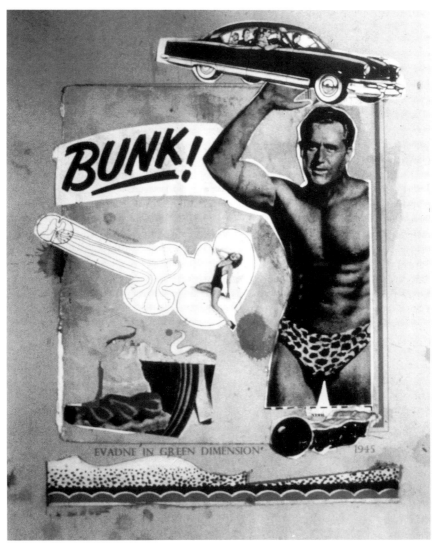

**44]** Eduardo Paolozzi, *Bunk* (1971). This series of screenprints was originally research material gathered by the artist during his stay in Paris

That there are quite a few facts that need to be put right is less to the point than the need to warn against the ingenuousness of many art historians and critics in the trust they place upon eye-witnesses notoriously the least reliable testimony one can find as Peter Hain could tell them.[38]

Despite such discerning comments, del Renzio relied upon Alloway's version of events:

during the Sixties there was a current in English art in which some of the brightest talents participated and which, almost alone, achieved the high reputation of English art. That current was the result of a build-up during the Fifties. The Independent Group more than any other gathering of artists, critics, historians, intellectuals, contributed decisively to that build-up.[39]

Not only has Alloway's version of events been assimilated into art historical accounts, but into examinations of popular culture too. In the light of hindsight, the Group is often hailed as a far-sighted elite, who not only foresaw the emergence of British Pop, but also the social and cultural changes which became manifest only in the 1960s. Christopher Booker wrote in 1969:

The Teddy Boys, the jazz fans, the Independent Group, were only tiny minorities, the Festival of Britain soon nothing but a fading memory. But they were symptoms that, even in those bleak post-war days, there was already a handful of people in Britain who were beginning to catch glimpses of a very different world – an enticing, far-off New World, of shining buildings, gaudy advertisements, chromium-plated cars, flashing lights and pulsating, thrilling music, a world of untold freedom and excitement.[40]

George Melly, in *Revolt into Style*, made a less extravagant, but equally significant claim: 'in fact the ICA group were a year or two in advance of the teenage revolution.'[41]

This assessment of the significance of the Independent Group displays not only an unquestioning acceptance of the myth, as proposed by Alloway, but an application of its meaning to a wider context. Dick Hebdige stressed a similar theme in his article 'In Poor Taste':

an embryonic study of popular culture focussing on the conflict between popular aspirations and entrenched interests (taste makers) and proposing a model of cultural consumption which stresses class and regional differences was already being developed – albeit somewhat intuitively – by Alloway, Hamilton, McHale and the Smithsons during the mid to late 50s.[42]

Not only does the preceding quote belie an acceptance of Alloway's writing, but more obviously it relates to Banham. Whilst Alloway's narration tends to provide the basis for many mainstream accounts of the beginning of British Pop, that of Banham gained increasing approval amongst academics during the 1970s and 1980s. Simon Wilson, a member of the staff of the Education Department of the Tate Gallery, has written: 'British Pop art grew out of a whole generation's rejection of upper-class culture and out of a revolt within the art education system itself'. Wilson also cites Richard Morphet, author of the 1970 Richard Hamilton Tate catalogue, in support of the argument:

Important roots of British Pop art lie in the anti-elitist attitudes of a generation whose daily life in their formative years steeped them exceptionally thoroughly in their eventual source material, the admass culture of modern life.[43]

Whilst Banham has always eschewed academicism in his writing, his ideas have become increasingly accepted amongst art and design historians. *Theory and Design in the First Machine Age* is virtually a standard text in design and architectural history. Dr P. A. Sparke's doctoral thesis, *Theory and Design in the Age of Pop*, contains a detailed analysis of Banham's approach to design.[44] A further standard text on the design history undergraduate's booklist is Charles Jencks' *Modern Movements in Architecture*, originally a Ph.D. thesis written under the supervision of Reyner Banham. The seventh chapter of the thesis, *Recent British Architecture: Pop-Non-Pop*, examines the 'IG breaking the thresholds'.[45] Jencks proposed that:

If one were to pigeon-hole the scene of recent British architecture in a single metaphor it would have to be 'battlefield', and 'scarred battlefield' at that, for it is saturated with the shellholes of polemic.[46]

This is a polemic in which the Independent Group, and particularly Banham, has been involved at every stage.

Whilst Banham's novel approach contributed extensively to the new discipline of design history, particularly through the seminal work of Penny Sparke, his version of the myth of the Independent Group has elicited a similar response amongst Marxists. British Marxist critiques of culture were overhauled by an introduction of Antonio Gramsci's theory of hegemony during the 1980s. First formulated in his *Prison Notebooks* of 1926 to 1937, and published in English in 1971,[47] Gramsci's theory constituted a challenge to accepted or 'vulgar' Marxism. Gramsci could not accept the Marxist premise that those activities which constituted the superstructure of a society were mere reflections of a determining base structure. Prompted by the revolution which had taken place in mass communications since the nineteenth century and the manner in which it could be exploited to gain or hold political power, as in the case of Italian Fascism, Gramsci assigned a much more important role to the superstructure of society, replacing it with the concept of hegemony.

By hegemony Gramsci meant the permeation throughout civil society – including a whole range of structures and activities such as trade unions, schools, the churches, and the family – of an entire system of values, attitudes, beliefs, morality etc., that is in one way or another supportive of the established order and the class interests that dominate it.[48] Furthermore the hegemony of any given society is not static but in a permanent state of flux, not because of economic factors, but because of opposing political and cultural ideas. Hence, hegemony accords significantly more importance to the role of the intellectual than previous Marxist theory has allowed. Hegemony played a vital role in the influential Open University's U203 *Popular Culture* course, for example: 'This view accords special importance to the role of intellectuals in the construction, as well as the contestation, of hegemony.'[49]

Dick Hebdige has been one of the first cultural historians to utilise hegemony in a full-length study, published in 1979 on the subject of *Subculture: The Meaning of Style*. Hebdige has also endeavoured to apply the concept of hegemony to the myth of the Independent Group, in his article 'In Poor Taste' included in the July 1983 issue of *Block*. He makes certain assumptions about the Independent Group which are drawn from the myth and takes it for granted that the Independent Group consisted of provincial, working-class or lower middle-class products of the new education system. According to Hebdige Pop Art was 'Art's sacred vessel seized by a gang of low-born pirates.'[50] This has also been the view propounded by Banham, which fits snugly into the Marxist framework of culture and society. Apparently the dominant ideology of post-war Britain was challenged, within the realms of culture, by the alienated members of the Independent Group. Because the myth of the Independent Group, especially as recounted by Banham, proves the Marxist theory to be relevant, the material itself is not questioned.

During the later 1980s and 1990s the academic study of culture has been immensely influenced by the writing of French, postmodern critics, particularly Pierre Bourdieu and J-F. Lyotard. This has led to a greater affirmation of the significance of the Independent Group within Cultural Studies. For example, Graeme Turner in *British Cultural Studies: An Introduction* (1990) discusses its importance in terms of a peripheral 'other', beyond the mainstream of this academic area. Even Turner's summary of the Independent Group is based – via Iain Chambers's *Popular Culture: The Metropolitan Experience* (1986) – on the Hebdige and Alloway accounts. A recent spate of exhibitions has served to reinforce the myth of the Independent Group including *The Sixties Art Scene in London* of 1993 where the Group is, yet again, regarded as the launching point for Pop Art and the 'natural' beginning of British Pop without question. The same could be said of the book, tellingly entitled *Modern Dreams: The Rise and Fall of Pop* (1988), the result of an exhibition held at The Institute for Contemporary Art, The

Clocktower Gallery, New York. The most recent manifestation of the myth was the ICA exhibition, *The Independent Group: Postwar Britain and The Aesthetics of Plenty*, which celebrated the Independent Group's proto-Pop concerns as well as their supposed proto-post-modernist leanings in 1990. In the undigested conglomoration of material which makes up the catalogue there is scant mention of the ICA as a seminal force for the founding and survival of the Group nor is the question of cultural context, modernism or design discussed – and the question of the Cold War is certainly never raised. The central focus remains the Group's influence on succeeding generations of Pop artists.

## Notes

1  L. Alloway, 'Notes on Abstract Art and the Mass Media', *Art News and Review*, 27 February to 12 March 1960, p. 12. Reyner Banham mentioned the Independent Group several times in the footnotes of his article 'Industrial Design e arte popolare', which appeared in *Civiltà delle Macchine*, November 1955. However, as the article only appeared in Italy, it did not contribute towards the myth of the Independent Group.

2  Dorothy Morland in an interview with the author, 6 September 1983.

3  R. Banham, From the script of *Primitives of a Mechanised Art* broadcast on BBC Third Programme, 21 November 1959, BBC Archives.

4  From the script of *Artists as Consumers: The Splendid Bargain* broadcast 11 March 1960 on BBC Third Programme, BBC Archives.

5  L. Alloway, 'Notes on Abstract Art and the Mass Media'.

6  L. Alloway, 'The Development of British Pop' in L. Lippard, *Pop Art*. Thames & Hudson, 1978, p. 201.

7  L. Alloway, 'Notes on Abstract Art and the Mass Media', p. 12.

8  *Ibid*.

9  The discussion was summarised in *Art News and Review*, 26 January 1952.

10  Lawrence Alloway was Curator of the Solomon R. Guggenheim Museum from 1962 to 1966.

11  R. Banham, *World of Books*, broadcast on BBC Third Programme, 14 February 1967, BBC Archives.

12  R. Melville, *Studio* 172, November 1966, unpaginated supplement.

13  The *Young Contemporaries* exhibition of 1961 included work by Barrie Bates (later Billy Apple), Derek Boshier, Patrick Caulfield, David Hockney, Allen Jones, R. B. Kitaj, Peter Phillips and Norman Toynton, who made their first impact as Pop artists in London.

14  BBC Audience Research Report, undated, p. 1, BBC Archives.

15  R. Banham, 'Who Is This Pop?', *Motif*, winter 1962/3, p. 13.

16  L. Alloway, 'Pop Art Since 1949', *The Listener*, 27 December 1962, p. 1087.

17  L. Alloway, 'The Development of British Pop', p. 40.

18  R. Banham, 'New Brutalism', *Architectural Review*, December 1955, p. 356.

19  *Ibid*., p. 357.

**20** R. Banham, 'Vision in Motion', *Art*, January 1955, p. 3.

**21** R. Banham, 'The Atavism of the Short-Distance Mini-Cyclist', *Living Arts*, No. 3, 1964, p. 91.

This article was initially a lecture, delivered by Banham at the ICA in autumn, 1963 as the Terry Hamilton Memorial Lecture. This means that the original audience for Banham's material would have been familiar with the Independent Group, and some of the audience may even have been members, hence ensuring an informed and positive response.

**22** R. Banham, 'The Atavism of the Short-Distance Mini-Cyclist', p. 92.

**23** The Smithsons were dissatisfied with this account of New Brutalism largely because it contained so many inaccuracies. They recorded their objections in a substantial review, '"Banham's Bumper Book on Brutalism" discussed by Alison and Peter Smithson', *Architects Journal*, 28 December 1966, p. 1590.

**24** R. Banham, 'The Detroit Tin Re-Visited' in *Design 1900–1960 – Studies in Design and Popular Culture*, Newcastle upon Tyne Polytechnic, 1976, p. 127.

**25** J. Reichardt, 'Pop Art and After', *Art International*, February 1963, pp. 42–7.

**26** *Ibid.*, p. 43.

**27** *Ibid.*

**28** R. Hamilton, *Collected Words*, Thames & Hudson, 1982, p. 28.

**29** D. Sylvester, 'Art in a Coke Climate', *Sunday Times Colour Supplement*, 26 January 1964, p. 14.

**30** For example, Sylvester analysed the symbolism of the Rolls-Royce within the criteria of expendability and new technology:

The design of the Rolls Royce radiator is intended to evoke the pediment and columns of the Parthenon and also those of all the banks and museums that already have evoked the Parthenon. The radiator thereby symbolises permanence, dignity, silence and wealth.

The Rolls Royce pretends that technology can be integrated into a wine culture: it tries to establish a respectable continuity with the ancient world.

D. Sylvester, 'Art in a Coke Climate', p. 17.

**31** H. Osborne (ed.), *The Oxford Companion to Art*, Oxford University Press, 1970, p. 894. In this brief entry on the Independent Group, they are referred to as 'the Independence Group'.

**32** P. & L. Murray, *The Penguin Dictionary of Art and Artists*, Penguin, 1978, p. 356. Although this entry does not mention the Independent Group, it does utilise Alloway's theory of the three phases, and names Paolozzi and Hamilton as the originators of British Pop.

**33** E. Lucie-Smith, *Movements in Art Since 1945*, Thames & Hudson, 1969, pp. 133–4.

**34** J. Russell and S. Gablik, *Pop-Art Re-Defined*, Thames & Hudson, 1969, included L. Alloway, 'The Long Front of Culture' and J. McHale, 'The Fine Arts and the Mass Media'.

**35** F. Whitford, 'Paolozzi and the Independent Group' in Tate Gallery catalogue, *Eduardo Paolozzi*, 1971, p. 46.

**36** Anthony d'Offay exhibition catalogue, *Nigel Henderson*, 1977, p. 10.

**37** R. Hamilton, *Collected Words*, p. 10.

**38** T. del Renzio, 'Pop', *Art and Artists*, August 1976, p. 15.

**39** T. del Renzio, 'Pop', p. 19.

**40** C. Booker, *The Neophiliacs*, Collins, 1969, p. 38.

**41**  G. Melly, *Revolt Into Style*, Penguin, 1969, p. 15.

**42**  D. Hebdige, 'In Poor Taste', *Block*, No. 8, 1983, p. 67.

**43**  S. Wilson, *Pop*, Thames & Hudson, 1978, p. 34.

**44**  P. Sparke, Unpublished thesis, *Theory and Design in the Age of Pop*, Brighton Polytechnic, October 1975.

**45**  C. Jencks, *Modern Movements in Architecture*, Penguin, 1973, p. 270.

**46**  *Ibid.*, p. 239.

**47**  Translated into English in: Quintin Hoare and Geoffrey Nowell-Smith (eds), *Selections from the Prison Notebooks of Antonio Gramsci*, Lawrence and Wishart, 1971.

**48**  C. Boggs, *Gramsci's Marxism*, Pluto Press Ltd., 1980, p. 39.

**49**  T. Bennett, 'Popular Culture and Hegemony in Post-War Britain', Unit 18 of Open University U203 Course, *Popular Culture*, 1981, p. 18.

**50**  D. Hebdige, 'In Poor Taste', p. 55.

# 9

# The knowing consumer: the Independent Group and post-modernism

THE MOST significant achievements of the Independent Group were a reworking of modernism, a revision of the role of the consumer and a re-evaluation of the high/low culture divide. These are themes which closely relate to the post-modernist debate. The emergence of post-modernism since the 1970s has led to a nascent recognition of the contribution of the Independent Group to the understanding of culture beyond the baton-passing model of art history. The field of Cultural Studies, where the Group's work has most relevance, has recently given some scant recognition of its contribution but this understanding is informed by the writing of Dick Hebdige which in turn is drawn from the myth constructed by Alloway. There is also a danger that the parallels between the Group's thinking and post-modernism may be too closely drawn, as in the case of the 1990 *Aesthetics of Plenty* exhibition.[1] The Group certainly re-evaluated modernism but did not propose that it should be superseded. They declared an alternative critique of the modern movement but remained devotees of Dada, Josef Albers and Jackson Pollock. But why has the recognition of the Independent Group taken so long and why is it so scant? The foundations of Cultural Studies were essentially literary rather than visual. Moreover, the Independent Group proposed a positive analysis of mass culture from within – as knowing consumers who found pleasure in going to the cinema – an approach which remains largely unacceptable amongst academics.

The first major contribution of the Independent Group to an analysis of culture is its dismantling of the traditional hierarchy which placed fine art and worthy literature above design and the mass media. Writers on culture since Matthew Arnold's *Culture and Anarchy* (1869) have established the primacy of high culture over low culture. During the ascendancy of Hollywood in the 1930s literary critic Q. D. Leavis demolished popular literature in *Fiction and the Reading Public* (1932) and Denys Thompson did the same of advertising in *Culture and Environment* (1933). Similar thinking informed both the founding of the ICA and the discipline of Cultural Studies. Endemic within early Cultural Studies was a distinct anti-Americanism. Mass or low culture equalled American imports, whether they be television, advertising, consumer products, music, film or lifestyle. A classic example of this approach is Richard Hoggart's *The Uses of Literacy* (1958) where he described the 'Juke Box Boy' – as a 'hedonistic but passive barbarian'.[2] Hoggart was lamenting the disappearance of his own working-class, Leeds childhood with its emphasis on the community and indigenous popular culture. Banham was immensely critical of the Hoggart approach, particularly during the later 1950s when he took up a regular slot in the 'Arts and Entertainment' section of the *New Statesman* from 1958 until the mid-1960s. In a 1962 review of Stirling and Gowan's development at Avenham in Preston entitled 'Coronation Street, Hoggartsborough' he criticised those 'sentimental socialists who read the *Uses of Literacy* as a plea to put the clock back.' Banham regarded modern design as serving the community, supplying new mechanical services like indoor toilets and decent heating. He saw Hoggart as the patronising admirer of 'picturesque peasantry'.[3] Banham was certainly identified by the emerging Cultural Studies group as an admirer of the detestable American mass culture. In the sixth issue of *New Left Review* M. Neufeld reviewed Banham's *Theory and Design in the First Machine Age* and criticised the author for:

appearing to lend support to that group of fashionable young architects who glory in the age of the ad-man, who profess an admiration for the vulgar forms of American motor cars and juke-boxes.[4]

This view was ironically shared by the reactionary connoisseurs' magazine, *Apollo*, in a review of *This is Tomorrow* which deplored the entire show, deriding it as 'pretentious bunk'. The critic's parting shot is particularly revealing:

May I add that quite ceaselessly a juke-box (that beloved tune creator sacred to the pin-table saloon) screams the poorest kind of popular contemporary music.[5]

Therefore, left and right alike were not in agreement with the Independent Group's position during the 1950s, both guarding the strict delineation between quality 'high' and 'low' culture. Banham recognised this contradiction in 1961 when reviewing the development of design theory over the past ten years:

Thus a narrowly Stalinist frame of reference, rigidly maintained beyond its last point of utility, has resulted in the sterility and subsequent disappearance of radical left-wing design criticism in Western democracies, and leaves intelligent socialists, like Richard Hoggart, apparently sharing the opinions of an 'Establishment' that they otherwise despise.[6]

Since the 1960s writers have tended to turn the high/low culture divide on its head and assume a populist approach. For example, Jim McGuigan in *Cultural Populism* (1992) writes of 'any form of culture that appeals to ordinary people could reasonably, in my view, be called "populist culture" with no necessarily evaluative judgement implied.'[7] For the Independent Group it was essential to evaluate the workings of mass culture, to judge why one image was more effective than another, to affirm the skill of the graphic designer or marketeer in creating an advertisement. Mass culture was worthy of just as much serious attention as high culture. In a provocative pair of articles, 'The expendable ikon 1' and 'The expendable ikon 2' in 1959, John McHale offered a serious analysis of successful visual communication drawn from the American mass media. He analysed *Mad* magazine as successful satire, Elvis as powerful totem in contemporary myth and *Double Your Money* as a sophisticated, ritual drama. For McHale these were the best examples of mass culture in 1959. He would not indiscriminately analyse any aspect of the mass media. The important point to bear in mind is that the Independent Group saw itself as knowing consumers, as analysing mass culture from within as people who had grown up with Hollywood and American comic books. Its view of the consumer was one of a sophisticated reader of complex imagery and not the passive sap of Cultural Studies. The Group certainly regarded design as satisfying consumer needs which were not dictated by the media, but by personal desires and dreams. Banham wrote in 'The End of Insolence' in the *New Statesman* of 1960:

And how can you condemn public taste as 'low' without adopting a position of snobbery intolerable in a liberal, let alone a socialist? The concept of good design as a form of aesthetic charity done on the labouring poor from a great height is incompatible with democracy as I see it. We need, instead, a concept of good design as the radical solution to the problem of satisfying consumer needs.[8]

Here the Independent Group's perspective tallies with one of the leading theorists of consumption, Dr Colin Campbell. In his seminal publication on the subject, *The Romantic Ethic and the Spirit of Modern Consumption* he argues that modern consumption serves the needs of individual day-dreams which are not mechnically determined by economics or status. Products are aids to constructing private dreams, the 'material of illusory enjoyment.'[9] It is the concept of enjoyment and pleasure which has been missing from mainstream Cultural Studies in its pursuit of ideological explanations of mass culture and the manipulation of consumers, out of touch with their 'real' needs. In the Introduction to the *Man, Machine and Motion* catalogue Richard Hamilton and Lawrence Gowing wrote of the pleasures of motorcycling:

The relation between man and machine is a kind of union, the two act together like a single creature. The ancient union of horse and rider, fused into a composite creature with an unruly character of its own, always potentially anarchic and fearsome, never entirely predictable, was symbolised in the myth of the centaur. The new union of man and machine possesses as positive a composite character and liberates a deeper, more fearsome human impulse. This new affiliation, evoking much that is heroic and much that is terrible, is with us, not only in the sky, but in every street where a boy joins magically with his motor-bicycle, his face whipped by the wind and stiffened by a passion for which we have no name.[10]

Hamilton's positive analysis of the relationship between rider and motorcycle is echoed in the remainder of the Independent Group's writing. Toni del Renzio in 'After a fashion . . .' discusses fashion illustration as 'the folk-art of a technological age, the visualising of the emotional experiences and realisable dreams of the mass-audience.'[11] At the 1960 National Union of Teachers Conference on *Popular Culture and Personal Responsibility* Hamilton spoke of the artist as consumer in an event which generally set the anti-mass media agenda of Cultural Studies for the ensuing thirty years: 'It seems to me that the artist, the intellectual, is not the alien that he was and his consumption of popular culture is due, in some measure, to his new role as a creator of popular culture.'[12] And this is what distinguishes the Independent Group. It is its essential involvement in all aspects of mass culture as opposed to the normal, academic disdain for the whole process. The Group was unique in its respect for the mass media. Many of the members were working within the media by the later 1950s: Toni del Renzio as Art Editor of *Harper's Bazaar* from 1958, Frank Cordell as a producer of popular music and Reyner Banham as a journalist. They are still virtually unique in the 1990s. For example, their interest in science fiction has remained unrecognised. A recent study of the subject argues that 'The comics were indefensible. They must have been, since no one defended them. They were universally condemned.'[13] Because the emphasis of Cultural Studies has been on the Marxist model, then those working within the media or contented consumers of it, are regarded as unwitting pawns within the capitalist mode of production. As Geoffrey Wagner noted in 1954: 'My view is simply that Americans are being imposed upon by those responsible for the production of drivel.'[14]

Hamilton's conviction about the importance of mass culture inspired his fine art work during the later 1950s and 1960s. Often accompanied by detailed accounts of his sources which were taken from advertising in mass circulation magazines, they raised important questions about how visual communication works in the mass media. For example, the production of *$he* was enhanced by the article, 'An exposition of $he' in *Architectural Design* (October 1962). Hamilton reveals his sources for the artwork as ten American adverts for fridges and small, domestic gadgets. He amalgamates the references into a subtle painting with multilayered meaning (Figure 45). The layout derives from an advert for an RCA Whirlpool fridge/freezer, the pink of the fridge from Cadillacs of the time, the cut-out plywood shape signified the famous back of model Vikky Dougan whilst also relating to the outline of an apron. In this work Hamilton refers to different methods of visual communication – the diagram, with the train of dots signifying the passage of toast as it pops up – the photograph and traditional painting techniques. Multilayered meanings were to inform other work of a similar period using similar sources, for example *Hommage à Chrysler Corp* (1957, Figure 46), *Hers is a Lush Situation* (1958, Figure 47) and *AAH* (1962, Figure 48).

Whilst such an open approach to mass culture may appear to lend itself to post-modernism it should also be borne in mind that the Group re-evaluated modernism rather than superseded it. Hamilton's art work throughout the later 1950s and early 1960s may have included references to the mass media, but there were also important references to modernism and the work of Marcel Duchamp in particular. Note the appearance of the United Nations building in *Hers is a Lush Situation* as a windscreen. The works of the later 1950s were also informed by Hamilton's ongoing production of a typographic version of Duchamp's *Green Box* which was published in 1960. Links between type and image, diagrammatic devices and words were foremost in the artist's mind at the time of the production of his art works. Likewise Reyner Banham was writing critical

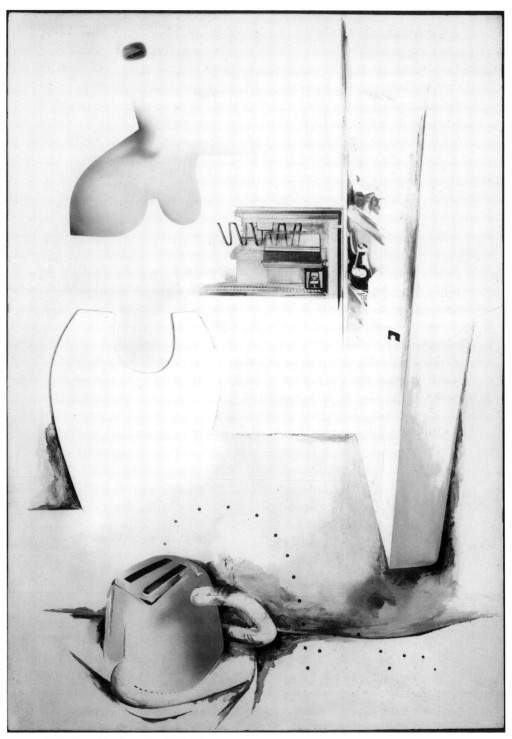

**45]** Richard Hamilton, *$he* (1958–61)

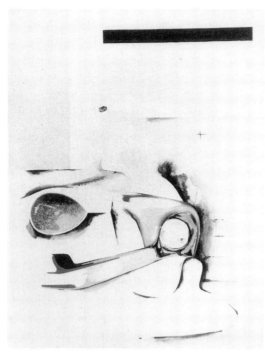

**46]** Richard Hamilton, *Hommage à Chrysler Corp* (1957)

**47]** Richard Hamilton, *Hers is a Lush Situation* (1958)

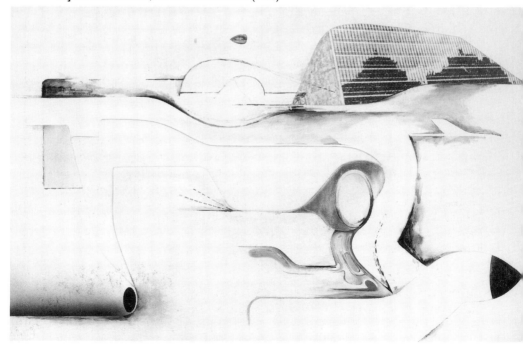

appreciations of modern masters such as Adolf Loos. In 'Ornament and Crime: The Decisive Contribution of Adolf Loos' Banham argues that the undecorated appearance of modern architecture came as a result of the writing of Loos which had been unacknowledged to date. Although Banham did not personally agree with Loos's 'peasant streak so common in reformist aesthetes'[15] he defended his contribution to the creation of modernism. Banham and the Independent Group's view of culture was all-embracing. As he argued in 'A Throw-Away Aesthetic' (Figures 49 and 50) in 1960:

The critic . . . must have the ability to sell the public to the manufacturer, the courage to speak out in the face of academic hostility, the knowledge

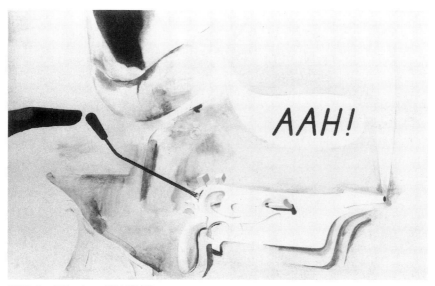

**48]** Richard Hamilton, *AAH* (1962)

to decide where, when and to what extent the standards of the popular arts are preferable to those of the fine arts. He must project the future dreams and desires of people as one who speaks from within their ranks. It is only thus that he can participate in the extraordinary adventure of mass-production, which counters the old aristocratic and defeatist 19th-century slogan, 'Few, but roses', and its implied corollary, 'Multitudes are weeds', with a new slogan that cuts across all academic catagories: 'Many, because orchids.'[16]

Therefore, in attempting to map out the achievements of the Independent Group against post-modernism there are certain important disparities. The re-evaluation of modernism with special focus on Adolf Loos, Dada and Marcel Duchamp; the retention of

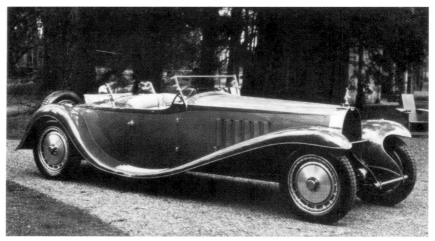

**49]** Bugatti, Royale Type 41, designed by Jean Bugatti, c. 1931

notions of quality in mass culture; and the pleasure of the process of consumption are three areas which do not directly correlate to post-modernism. The key points of post-modernity – a general loss of authority, fragmentation, surface as opposed to essential meaning, feminist or black perspectives, are simply nowhere to be found in the work of the Independent Group. What is apparent is something all-embracing and fundamentally usable. A complete and optimistic acceptance of mass and high culture in the twentieth century. It is only when a more inclusive account, such as this, of the Independent Group is attempted that the value of its contribution to rethinking culture can be fully realised. As Banham himself stated in 1977:

**50]** Buick Century de Luxe Riviera Sedan (1956), in contrast to Figure 47

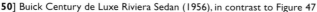
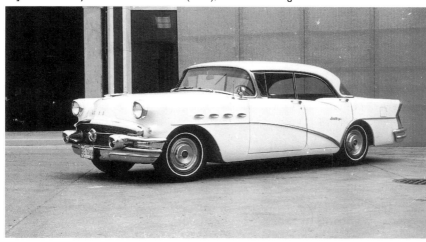

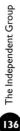

as far as the world's view of what happened is concerned, the importance of the Independent Group is that it made British Pop Art. . . . But in the process of saying that and accepting that, that may be the ultimate historical judgement. As always happens with historical judgements something like 95% of the Independent Group's actual activities goes in the discard bin. All the conversations about high technology, all the conversations about problems of art history, all the conversations on philosophical topics . . . go(es) overboard.[17]

## Notes

1  See, for example, David Robbins 'The Independent Group: Forerunners of Postmodernism' in *The Independent Group: Postwar Britain and the Aesthetics of Plenty*, exhibition catalogue, Hood Museum of Art, Dartmouth College, 1990, pp. 237–46.
2  R. Hoggart, *The Uses of Literacy*, Penguin, Harmondsworth, 1958, p. 250.
3  R. Banham, 'Coronation Street, Hoggartsborough', *New Statesman*, 9 February 1962, p. 200.
4  M. Neufeld, 'Theory and Design in the First Machine Age', *New Left Review*, No. 6, 1960, p. 71.
5  'Shaft from Apollo's Bow: This is Tomorrow – or is it?', *Apollo*, No. 64, September 1956, p. 89.
6  R. Banham, 'Design by Choice' in *Architectural Review*, July 1961, reprinted in P. Sparke (ed.) *Design by Choice*, Academy Editions, 1981, pp. 97–8.
7  J. McGuigan, *Cultural Populism*, Routledge, 1992, p. 2.
8  R. Banham, 'The End of Insolence' in *New Statesman*, 29 October 1960. Reprinted in P. Sparke, *Design by Choice*, pp. 121–3.
9  C. Campbell, *The Romantic Ethic and the Spirit of Modern Consumerism*, first published 1987, Balckwell, Oxford, 1993, p. 93.
10  L. Gowing and R. Hamilton, Preface to *Man, Machine and Motion* exhibition catalogue, Hatton Gallery, University of Newcastle, 1955, p. 2.
11  T. del Renzio, 'After a fashion', ICA Publications 2, 1958, unpaginated.
12  R. Hamilton, 'Art and Design' delivered at the NUT Conference, *Popular Culture and Personal Responsibility*, 1960. Reprinted in R. Hamilton, *Collected Words*, Thames & Hudson, 1982.
13  M. Barker, *A Haunt of Fears*, Pluto Press, 1984, p. 9.
14  G. Wagner, *A Parade of Pleasure*, 1954, p. 13.
15  R. Banham, 'Ornament and Crime: The Decisive Contribution of Adolf Loos', *Architectural Review*, February 1957, p. 86.
16  R. Banham, 'A Throw-away Aesthetic', *Industrial Design*, March 1960. Reprinted in P. Sparke, *Design by Choice*, p. 93.
17  R. Banham, *Fathers of Pop*, (discussion between Toni del Renzio, Richard Hamilton and Banham), 1977, p. 3.

# Appendix 1: *Aesthetic Problems of Contemporary Art*

## COURSE OF NINE SEMINARS ORGANISED BY THE ICA (1953–54)

### The aims of the course

It has been evident for some time that a demand exists, outside the ICA, as well as within its membership, for a more general discussion of the aesthetics of contemporary art than can usually be found in English criticism, which, for sound reasons of its own, prefers to deal with particular and technical problems of one art at a time.

It would be difficult to deal with these general problems in separate, independent lectures because their exact delimitation is inevitably vague, and the solution has appeared to be a course of seminars (more flexible than lectures in form) linked together by the continuous presence of the same chairman, Mr Robert Melville, whose place, when he is speaking, will be taken by the Registrar, Mr Reyner Banham, who will also be present throughout. The course, taken as a whole (as it is intended to be taken) though not utterly exhaustive should give the serious student a general picture (though not a detailed one) of the problems confronting the plastic arts in the 1950s.

The course will meet at fortnightly intervals, with a longer break at Christmas, on Thursdays at 8.15 p.m., commencing on 15 October. The order of speaking given below is approximate only, but members of the course will have good notice of any variations in the order.

# Speakers, with main heading of their subjects

### 15 October    Mr Reyner Banham
*The impact of technology*

The technological approach – the application of scientific discoveries to practical ends – as a characteristic mental attitude of the mid-century; its effect on the subject matter of art through the mechanisation of the environment, and on the status of the work of art itself, through the growth of techniques of mass reproduction.

### 29 October    Mr Richard Hamilton
*New sources of form*

The growth of new canons of form through the continual extension of our visual horizon under the impact of micro-photography, long range astronomy etc. Relevance of the forms so discovered to contemporary design procedures and to mathematical laws of structures and of statistics.

### 12 November    Mr Fello Atkinson, Mr William Turnbull
*New concepts of space*

The two speakers will divide the subject between themselves as between space experienced inside structures, and space as existing inside a work of art, respectively. The two concepts – of real and of fictive space – are by no means irreconcilable as at present understood since both depend from the separation of the idea of volume from the idea of solid mass, the latter being replaced by ideas of penetrability and transparency.

### 26 November    Mr C. A. St John Wilson
*Proportion and symmetry*

Recent mathematical and scientific research has shown the existence of certain far-reading laws of systematic proportion and forms of symmetry in nature; the application of these laws as a discipline or control in the plastic arts; the Modulor of Le Corbusier.

### 10 December    Mr Toni del Renzio
*Non-formal painting*

This subject, the only one relating to a single art, is introduced because it brings out the nature of the crisis which now faces many branches of the plastic arts: a crisis of signification, shifting the value of the work of art from the thing signified, to the act of signification itself, bringing to a head certain latent tendencies of abstract art hitherto held in check by formal preconceptions; abolition of classical ideas of a closed pictorial composition.

The following dates will be announced in due course

**Dr Johannes Brengelmann**
*Problems of perception*

The eye no longer regarded as a neutral reporter of the thing seen but as selective interpreter of visual stimuli; mechanisms of selection and perception; variations in interpretation of visual stimuli between individuals and between different physical and psychological conditions of the same person.

**Mr Laurence Alloway**
*The human image*

Factors affecting the return of the human image in contemporary art; new attitudes toward both 'man' and toward the concept 'image' produced by new factors – cinema, anthropology, archaeology – in contemporary life; relevance of these attitudes to other contemporary aspects of the plastic arts.

**Mr Robert Melville**
*Mythology and psychology*

Effects of recent research into the subconscious and the mythological on one another, and on the arts; ever-changing, but ever-vital effect of the art of alien cultures on our own; relevance of Surrealist and Dadaist discoveries in the realm of 'the wonderful'.

**Mr Reyner Banham**
*Summing up: Art in the fifties*

Apparent diversity of different tendencies masking many points of agreement; but no immediate prospect of uniformity or the appearance of any obviously uniform 'period-style'; true marks of genuinely contemporary manifestations lie in the absolutism of basic concepts, lack of compromise in pursuit of aims.

## Notes and directions

For technical reasons it will be necessary to limit the number of places on this course to just under 100, and preference in allocation of the places available will be given to members of the ICA, and to certain categories of students, for whom some places will be reserved until after the beginning of academic terms. These students to whom preference will be given are those at Art Schools, those studying the history of art, and bona fide students (and ex-students) of adult classes in the appreciation on history of art.

For ICA members, and the designated categories of students, the fee for the course will be £1, for others £1.7.6. No promises of seats for individual lectures can be entered into, but applications in writing *in advance* will be considered when the register is in hand.

Cards of membership of the course will only be issued against receipt of the application form enclosed, of which spare copies may be had from the ICA.

# Appendix 2: Independent Group Session 1955

The Independent Group of the Institute of Contemporary Arts was formed in 1952 as a forum for the opinions of the younger members of the Institute (under thirty-five years). Members included Nigel Herbert, William Turnbull, Lawrence Alloway, Peter Reyner Banham, Richard Hamilton, John McHale, Eduardo Paolozzi, Toni del Renzio, and Peter Smithson. Previously the IG had been convened by Reyner Banham to study techniques. Later in 1955 it was convened by Lawrence Alloway and John McHale for the purpose of investigating the relationship of the fine arts and popular art. The programme was not systematic but dependent on the current interests of the members who considered the IG as a trial ground for new ideas. From these closed meetings public lectures were subsequently developed.

**11 February 1955**

Paintings by Richard Hamilton. Discussion centred round the use of the photographically defined new reality (with a stress on popular serial imagery) in a fine art context; its legitimacy and effectiveness in relation to paintings as individual gestures. Main speakers: Richard Hamilton, John McHale, Reyner Banham, Lawrence Alloway.                    (Attendance 14)

**4 March 1955**

Borax, or the thousand horse-power mink by Reyner Banham. Borax equals, in this context, current automobile styling. Its theme (vide Plymouth ads) is Metal in Motion, expressed by an iconography which refers to, e.g. sports and racing cars, aviation, science fiction; all relevant to theme of transportation, but all exotic to the American automobile. Auxillary iconographies postulate brutalism, oral symbols and sex, emphasising that Borax is popular art, as well as a universal style (in US not in Europe) and sex-iconography establishes the automobile's dream rating – on the frontier of the dream that money can only just buy (speaker's abstract). (Given as public lecture, METAL IN MOTION, at ICA on 7 July.) (Attendance 18)

## 8 March 1955

Probability and information theory and their application to the visual arts by E. W. Meyer. The statistical model devised by Shannon and others to explain the particular case of the transmission of information in an electrical communication network has proved eminently successful, but its induction to the visual arts would appear difficult because of the hyperspherical dimensionality of the transmitter–medium–receiver complex (speaker's abstract). (Extensive use made of visual aids: diagrams, epidiascope projection, blackboard, gadgets.) (Attendance 22)

## 15 April 1955

Advertising, 1. A random, introspective survey of American advertisements with reference to the interplay of technology and social symbolism. Phantasy as a constant, topical presentation as a variable, received preliminary definition. Main speakers: Peter Smithson, Eduardo Paolozzi, John McHale, Lawrence Alloway. (Attendance 22)

## 29 April 1955

Dadaists as non-Aristotelians. The post-war Dada revival has contradicted history of the movement. Dada as anti-absolutist and multi-valued, like advertising lay-outs, movies, etc. An attempt was made to connect Dada with the non-Aristotelian logic of provisional probabilities. Main speakers: John McHale, Anthony Hill, Donald Holmes, Toni del Renzio. (Attendance 14)

## 27 May 1955

Advertising, 2. Sociology in the popular arts. Earlier attitudes to popular material criticised for aesthetic and moral prejudice. Intensive, multi-layered analysis of one advertisement as exemplar of descriptive method with 'performance as referent'. Main speakers: Lawrence Alloway, John McHale, Eduardo Paolozzi, Toni del Renzio. (Attendance 16)

## 24 June 1955

Fashion and fashion magazines by Toni del Renzio. Fashion is one of the popular arts peculiar to the age of technology. If its changes are not as rapid and as thorough as some mass media communications would indicate, nonetheless its changes contribute and correspond to the changing conceptual image of woman. Audrey Hepburn is a typical symbol caught in the rival and co-operative coding processes of the cinema and the other mass media – other-directed antagonistic co-operation (speaker's abstract). (Attendance 16)

## 1 July 1955

Aesthetics and Italian product design. Discussion between Gillo Dorfles and Reyner Banham. Dorfles represented topical Italian ideas about the complex relation to industrial design to traditional aesthetics. He proposed an external standard of taste by which both objects of fine art and objects of good 'non-art' could be judged. (Attendance 20)

## 15 July 1955

Gold Pan Alley by Frank Cordell. The popular song as one of the arts that has emerged from the seminal interaction of technology and mass communications. Millions of pounds are spent annually by music, radio, and recording industries in producing and selling this product and its pervasive power is such that hardly any group of individuals in the western world can remain untouched by its manifestations. A study of commercial music in its producer–consumer relationships provides a revealing index of certain cultural and sociological emphases in the contemporary situation. (Attendance 14)

# Bibliography

All material published in London unless otherwise stated.

## Books

Adams, H. *Art of the Sixties*, Phaidon, 1978

Alloway, L. *Nine Abstract Artists*, Alec Tiranti Ltd, 1954

Alloway, L. *The Metallization of a Dream*, Lion and Unicorn, 1963

Alloway, L. 'The Development of British Pop, in L. Lippard, *Pop Art*, Thames and Hudson, 3rd edn, pp. 26–7

Amaya, M. *Pop as Art: A Survey of the New Super-Realism*, Studio Vista, 1965

Banham, M. (ed.) *A Tonic to the Nation*, Thames and Hudson, 1977

Banham, R. *Theory and Design in the First Machine Age*, 1st edn, Architectural Press, 1966

Banham, R. *The New Brutalism: Ethic or Aesthetic?*, Architectural Press, 1966

Banham, R. *Design by Choice*, edited by Penny Sparke, Academy Editions, 1981

Barker, M. *A Haunt of Fears: The Strange History of the British Horror Comics Campaign*, Pluto Press, 1984

Barker, M. *Comics – Ideology, Power and the Critics*, Manchester University Press, 1989

Barthes, R. *Mythologies*, Paladin, 1973

Booker, C. *The Neophiliacs*, Collins, 1969

Boyle, A. *The Climate of Treason*, 2nd edn, Coronet Books, 1980

Boyne, R. and Rattansi, A. (eds) *Postmodernism and Society*, Macmillan, 1990

Bradbury, M. and McFarlane, J. (eds) *Modernism*, Penguin, 1976

Brill, R. *Modern Painting*, Avalon Press and Collins, 1946

Brumwell, J. R. M. (ed.) *This Changing World*, Readers Union, Routledge, 1945

Calvocoressi, P. *The British Experience, 1945–75*, Pelican, 1975

Carey, J. *The Intellectuals and the Masses: Pride and Prejudice among the Literary Intelligentsia 1880–1939*, Faber and Faber, 1992

Chambers, I. *Popular Culture: The Metropolitan Experience*, New York, 1986

Compton, M. *Pop Art*, Hamlyn, 1970

Cox, I. *The South Bank Exhibition: A Guide to the Story it Tells*, HMSO, 1951

Dorfles, G. *Kitsch*, Studio Vista, 1969

Evans, B. I. and Glasgow, M. *The Arts in England*, The Falcon Press, 1945

Finch, C. *Pop Art: Object as Image*, Studio Vista, 1968

Finch, C. *Image as Language: Aspects of British Art*, Penguin, 1969

Finlay, I. *Art in Scotland*, Oxford University Press, London, 1948

Fiske, J. *Understanding Popular Culture*, Unwin Hyman, 1989

Ford, H. *These were the Hours: Memoirs of My Hours Press, Reanville and Paris 1928–1931*, Fefffer and Simons, 1968

Gaunt, W. *British Painting, from Hogarth's Day to Ours*, Avalon Press Limited and Central Institute of Art and Design, 1945

Giedion, S. *Mechanization Takes Command*, W. W. Norton, New York, 1948

Guggenheim, P. *Out of this Century: Confessions of an Art Addict*, André Deutsch, 1980

Guilbaut, S. *How New York Stole the Idea of Modern Art: Abstract Expressionism, Freedom and the Cold War*, Chicago, The University of Chicago Press, 1983

Hall, S. and Whannel, P. *The Popular Arts*, Hutchinson, 1964

Hamilton, R. *Collected Words*, Thames and Hudson, 1982

Harrison, C. *English Art and Modernism, 1900–1939*, Allen Lane, 1981

Harrison, T. *Britain Revisited*, Gollancz, 1961

Hebdige, D. *Subculture: The Meaning of Style*, Methuen, 1979

Hewison, R. *In Anger: Culture in the Cold War, 1945–60*, Weidenfeld and Nicolson, 1981

Hillier, B. *Austerity, Binge: The Decorative Arts of the Forties and Fifties*, Studio Vista, 1975

HMSO, *Art and Industry: Report of the Committee Appointed by The Board of Trade Under the Chairmanship of Lord Gorell on the Production and Exhibition of Articles of Good Design and Every Day User*, 1932

HMSO, *Report by the Council for Art and Industry: The Working Class House: Its Furnishing and Equipment*, 1937

Hockney, D. *David Hockney*, Thames and Hudson, 1976

Hoggart, R. *The Uses of Literacy* (first published 1957), Penguin, 1973

Ironside, R. 'Painting Since 1939' in *Since 1939*, Longmans, Green and Co. Ltd, 1948

Jencks, C. *Modern Movements in Architecture*, Pelican, 1973

Johnstone, W. *Creative Art in Britain: From the Earliest Times to the Present*, Macmillan and Co. Ltd, 1950

Johnstone, W. *Points in Time*, Barrie and Jenkins, 1981

King, J. *The Last of the Moderns: A Life of Herbert Read*, Weidenfeld and Nicolson, 1990

Korzybski, A. C. *Science and Sanity: An Introduction to Non-Aristotelian Systems and General Semantics*, The International Non-Aristotelian Library Publishing Co., The Science Press Printing Co., Lancaster, Pennsylvania, 1933

Lambert, M. and Marx, E. *English Popular Culture*, Batsford, 1951

Lewis, P. *The 50s*, Heinemann, 1978

Livingstone, M. *Pop Art: A Continuing History*, Thames and Hudson, 1990

Lyotard, J. *The Postmodern Condition: a Report on Knowledge*, Manchester University Press, 1984

MacCarthy, F. *A History of British Design*, 2nd edn, George Allen and Unwin, Ltd, 1979

McGuigan, J. *Cultural Populism*, Routledge, 1992

McLuhan, H. M. *The Mechanical Bride: Folklore of Industrial Man* (first published in America in 1951), Routledge and Kegan Paul, 1967

Marwick, A. *British Society Since 1945*, Penguin, 1982

Marwick, A. *Culture in Britain Since 1945*, Basil Blackwell, Oxford, 1991

Massey, A. *Interior Design of the Twentieth Century*, Thames and Hudson, 1990 (reprinted 1994)

Mellor, D. *The Sixties Art Scene in London*, Phaidon, 1993

Melly, G. *Revolt into Style*, Penguin, 1969

Miller, D. *Material Culture and Mass Consumption*, Blackwell, 1987

Munnings, A. *An Artist's Life: The Second Burst: The Finish*, Readers Union, 1955

Ozenfant, A. *The Foundations of Modern Art*, Dover Publications, New York, 1952

Packard, V. *The Hidden Persuaders*, Longman, 1957

Payne, R. *Fabulous America*, Victor Gollancz, 1949

Penrose, R. *Scrap Book 1900–1981*, Thames and Hudson, 1981

Pevsner, N. *Pioneers of Modern Design* (first published by Faber and Faber in 1936), Penguin, 1977

Read, H. *The Future of Industrial Design*, a paper read before the DIA at Burlington House, 10 June 1943, published by DIA, 1946

Read, H. *Contemporary British Art*, Pelican, 1951

Read, H. *The Philosophy of Modern Art*, Faber and Faber, 1951

Riesman, D. *The Lonely Crowd* (first published in 1950), Yale University Press, New Haven, 1961

Rose, B. *American Art Since 1900*, 2nd edn, Thames and Hudson, 1975

Rothenstein, J. *Brave Day, Hideous Night*, Hamish Hamilton, 1966

Russell, J. and Gablik, S. *Pop Art Re-Defined*, Thames and Hudson, 1969

Schneede, U. M. *Paolozzi*, Thames and Hudson, 1971

Sissons, M. and French, P. (eds) *Age of Austerity*, Hodder and Stoughton, 1963

Sparke, P. (ed.) *Design by Choice*, Academy Editions, 1981

Spectorsky, A. C. *The Exurbanites*, J. B. Lippincott & Co., Philadelphia and New York, 1955

Spender, S. *The Thirties and After*, Fontana, 1978

Strinati, D. and Wagg, S. (eds) *Come On Down: Popular Media Culture*, Routledge, 1992

Tate Gallery, *Modern British Paintings, Drawings and Sculpture*, Oldbourne, 1964

Thompson, D. (ed.) *Discrimination and Popular Culture*, Penguin, 1964

Thompson, E. P. *The Poverty of Theory and Other Essays*, Merlin Press, 1978

Turner, G. *British Cultural Studies: An Introduction*, Routledge, 1992

Varnedoe, K. and Gopnik, A. (eds) *Modern Art and Popular Culture: Readings in High and Low*, Museum of Modern Art, New York, 1990

Walker, J. A. *Art in the Age of Mass Media*, Pluto Press, 1983

Walker, J. A. *Art Since Pop*, Woodbury, New York, 1978

Wallis, B. *Modern Dreams: The Rise and Fall and Rise of Pop*, New York, 1988

Warren, C. H. *England is a Village*, Eyre and Spottiswoode, 1941

Webster, D. *Looka Yonder!: the Imaginary America of Populist Culture*, Routledge, 1988

Whiteley, N. *Pop Design. Modernism to Mod*, London, 1987

Wilenski, R. H. *The Modern Movement in Art*, Faber and Faber, 1956

Wilson, S. *Pop*, Thames and Hudson, 1974

Wilson, S. *Pop Art*, London, 1974

Wollen, P. *Raiding the Icebox: Reflections on Twentieth Century Culture*, Verso, 1993

Yarsley, V. E. and Couzens, E. G. *Plastics*, Pelican, Middlesex, 1944

## Exhibition catalogues

Anthony d'Offay, *Nigel Henderson, Paintings, Drawings and Photographs*, catalogue of an exhibition, 1977

Anthony d'Offay, *Richard Hamilton, Drawings, Prints and Paintings, 1941–1955*, catalogue of an exhibition with an Introduction by Anne Seymour, 1980

Arts Council of Great Britain, *Portraits*, catalogue of an exhibition held at the Galleries of Messrs Wildenstein, London 1945 with a Foreword by Allan Gwynne-Jones

Arts Council of Great Britain, *60 Paintings for '51*, catalogue of a touring exhibition with a Foreword by Philip James, 1951

Arts Council of Great Britain, *Recent British Painting*, catalogue of a touring exhibition with a Foreword by John Commander, 1954

Arts Council of Great Britain, *Arts Council Collection: A Selection from the Oil Paintings, Part One*, catalogue of a touring exhibition with a Foreword by Philip James, 1955

Arts Council of Great Britain, *4 French Realists*, catalogue of a touring exhibition with an Introduction by Quentin Bell, 1955

Arts Council of Great Britain, *Ten Years of British Architecture*, catalogue of a touring exhibition with an Introduction by John Summerson, 1956

Arts Council of Great Britain, *Decade '40s*, catalogue of a touring exhibition with an Introduction by Alan Bowness, 1972

Arts Council of Great Britain, *Eduardo Paolozzi*, catalogue of a touring exhibition with a Foreword by Joanna Drew, 1976

Barbican Art Gallery, *Aftermath, France 1945–54: New Images of Man*, catalogue of an exhibition, 1982

Clocktower Gallery, Institute for Art and Urban Resources, *This is Tomorrow Today. The Independent Group and British Pop Art*. Reprinted in *Modern Dreams: The Rise and Fall of Pop*, New York, 1988

Fisher Fine Art Ltd. and National Museum of Wales, *The British Neo-Romantics 1935–1950*, catalogue of a touring exhibition with a Foreword by Peter Cannon-Brookes, 1983

Gardner Centre Gallery, William Gear, *Paintings 1964–1971*, catalogue of an exhibition containing an interview by Malcolm Davies, 1971

Gimpel Fils, *William Gear*, catalogue of an exhibition with a Foreword by A. D. B. Sylvester, 1948

Gimpel Fils, *William Gear*, catalogue of an exhibition with a Foreword by Philip James, 1961

Hanover Gallery, *Kenneth King, Eduardo Paolozzi and William Turnbull*, catalogue of an exhibition with an essay on Paolozzi and Turnbull by A. D. B. Sylvester, 1950

Hanover Gallery, *Magda Cordell*, catalogue of an exhibition with a Foreword by Lawrence Alloway, 1956

HMSO, *The South Bank: A Guide to the Story it Tells*, Official Guide to the Festival of Britain by Ian Cox, 1951

ICA, *40,000 Years of Modern Art*, catalogue of an exhibition, 1948

ICA, *Forty Years of Modern Art: 1907–1947, A Selection from British Collections*, catalogue of an exhibition with an Introduction by Herbert Read, 1948

ICA, *Graham Sutherland*, catalogue of an exhibition with a Foreword by Raymond Mortimer, 1951

ICA, *Growth and Form*, catalogue of an exhibition with a Foreword by Herbert Read, 1951

ICA, *Matta*, catalogue of an exhibition with a Foreword by Robert Melville, 1951

ICA, *Picasso, Drawings and Watercolours Since 1883*, exhibition catalogue with an essay, 'Homage to Picasso on his 70th Birthday' by Roland Penrose, 1951

ICA, *Ten Decades: A Review of British Taste, 1851–1951*, catalogue of an exhibition with an Introduction by Geoffrey Grigson, 1951

ICA, *Young Painters and Sculptors*, catalogue of an exhibition with a Foreword by Herbert Read, 1951

ICA, *Kokoschka*, catalogue of an exhibition with an Introduction by J. P. Hodin, 1952

ICA, *Recent Trends in Realist Painting*, catalogue of an exhibition with an Introduction by A. D. B. Sylvester, 1952

ICA, *Steinberg, Drawings*, catalogue of an exhibition, 1952

ICA, *Tomorrow's Furniture*, catalogue of an exhibition with an Introduction by Toni del Renzio, 1952

ICA, *Young Painters*, catalogue of an exhibition with a Preface by A. D. B. Sylvester, 1952

ICA, *Young Sculptors*, catalogue of an exhibition, 1952

ICA, *11 British Painters*, catalogue of an exhibition with an Introduction by Toni del Renzio, 1953

ICA, *Le Corbusier: Paintings, Drawings, Sculpture, Tapestry, 1918–1953*, catalogue of an exhibition with a Foreword by Colin St John Wilson, 1953

ICA, *Opposing Forces*, catalogue of an exhibition with a Foreword by Michel Tapie, translated by Peter Watson, 1953

ICA, *Parallel of Life and Art*, catalogue of an exhibition, 1953

ICA, *Wonder and Horror of the Human Head*, catalogue of an exhibition with a Foreword by Herbert Read and Roland Penrose, 1953

ICA, *Collages and Objects*, catalogue of an exhibition compiled by Lawrence Alloway, 1954

ICA, *Recent British Drawings*, catalogue of an exhibition with an Introduction by A. D. B. Sylvester, 1954

ICA, *Victor Pasmore: Paintings and Constructions, 1944–1954*, catalogue of an exhibition compiled by Lawrence Alloway, 1954

ICA, *A Continuing Process: The New Creativity in British Art Education 1955–1965*, catalogue of an exhibition compiled by David Thistlewood, 1981

King's College, University of Durham, *Man, Machine and Motion*, catalogue of an exhibition compiled by Richard Hamilton, Newcastle, 1955

Kunstverein, Hamburg, *Pop Art in England: Beginnings of a New Figuration 1947–63*, catalogue of a travelling exhibition, Hamburg, 1976

Mayor Gallery, *Eduardo Paolozzi*, catalogue of an exhibition, 1948

Mayor Gallery, *Eduardo Paolozzi*, catalogue of an exhibition, 1949

Museum of Modern Art, Oxford, *The Story of the AIA, 1933–1953*, catalogue of an exhibition compiled by Lynda Morris and Robert Radford, Oxford, 1983

Norwich School of Art, *Nigel Henderson*, catalogue of an exhibition with an Introduction by Bill English, Norwich 1982

O'Hana Gallery, *Dimensions*, catalogue of an exhibition compiled by Lawrence Alloway, 1957

Robbins, D. (ed.) *The Independent Group: Postwar Britain and the Aesthetics of Plenty*, catalogue of an exhibition held at the ICA London, Instituto Valenciano de Arte Moderno, Valencia, MCA, Los Angeles and Hood Museum of Art, California, 1990–1991

Royal Academy of Arts, London, *L'Ecole de Paris, 1900–1950*, catalogue of an exhibition with an Introduction by Jean Cassou, 1951

Sheffield City Art Galleries, *25 From '51: Paintings from the Festival of Britain*, catalogue of a touring exhibition with an Introduction by James Hamilton, Sheffield, 1978

Sheffield Arts Department, *The Forgotten Fifties*, catalogue of a travelling exhibition with a Preface by Julian Spalding, Sheffield, 1984

Tate Gallery, *The Unknown Political Prisoner*, catalogue of an exhibition of the prize-winners with an Introduction by Anthony J. T. Kloman, 1953

Tate Gallery, *Richard Hamilton*, catalogue of an exhibition, compiled by Richard Morphet, 1970

Tate Gallery, *Eduardo Paolozzi*, catalogue of an exhibition, compiled by Frank Whitford, 1971

Tate Gallery, *William Turnbull, Sculpture and Painting*, catalogue of an exhibition compiled by Richard Morphet, 1973

Tate Gallery, *Richard Hamilton*, 1992

Victoria and Albert Museum, *British Watercolours*, catalogue of an exhibition compiled by Graham Reynolds, 1951

Victoria and Albert Museum, *The Way We Live Now*, catalogue of an exhibition compiled by M. Timmer, 1978

Victoria and Albert Museum, *Photography in Printmaking*, catalogue of an exhibition compiled by Charles Newton, 1979

Whitechapel Art Gallery, *This is Tomorrow*, catalogue of an exhibition edited by Theo Crosby, 1956

Whitechapel Art Gallery, *British Sculpture in the Twentieth Century*, catalogue of an exhibition edited by Sandy Nairne and Nicholas Serota, 1981

## Articles

Alloway, L. 'Allegory and the Unconscious, Bronzino's "*Exposure of Luxury*"' in *Art News and Review*, 16 June 1951

Alloway, L. 'Britain's New Iron Age' in *Art News* (New York), summer 1953, pp. 18–20, 68–9

Alloway, L. 'A Decline in Klee?' in *Art News and Review 5*, 9 January 1954

Alloway, L. 'Art News from London' in *Arts News* (New York), May 1955, p. 11

Alloway, L. 'Graphics Annual and Modern Publicity, 1955–6' in *Encounter* March 1956, p. 94

Alloway, L. 'Technology and Sex in Science Fiction' in *Ark* No. 17, 1956, pp. 19–23

Alloway, L. 'London, Beyond Painting and Sculpture' in *Art News* (New York), September 1956, pp. 38, 64–5

Alloway, L. 'The Arts and the Mass Media' in *Architectural Design*, February 1958, pp. 84–5

Alloway, L. 'The Long Front of Culture' in *Cambridge Opinion*, No. 17, 1959 Reprinted in Russell, J. and Gablik, S., *Pop Art Redefined* (1969), pp. 41–3

Alloway, L. 'Notes on Abstract Art and the Mass Media' in *Art News and Review* 27 February–12 March 1960, pp. 3 and 12

Alloway, L. '"Pop Art" Since 1949' in *The Listener*, 27 December 1962, pp. 1085–87

Alloway, L. 'Popular Culture and Pop Art' in *Studio International*, July 1969, p. 16–21

Banham, R. 'The Shape of Everything' in *Art News and Review 3*, 14 July 1951, p. 2

Banham, R. 'Italian Eclectic' in *Art and Review 112*, October 1952, pp. 213–17

Banham, R. 'Parallel of Life and Art' in *Architectural Review*, October 1953, pp. 259–61

Banham, R. 'Paul Klee' in *Art News and Review 5*, 28 November 1953, p. 7

Banham, R. 'Klee's "Pedagogical Sketchbook"' in *Encounter*, 2 April 1954, pp. 53–8

Banham, R. 'Vision in Motion' in *Art*, 5 January 1955, p. 4

Banham, R. 'Eppur Si Muove' in *Art*, 17 February 1955, p. 4

Banham, R. 'Futurism' in *Art*, 3 March 1955, pp. 6 and 7

Banham, R. 'Machine Aesthetic' in *Architectural Review*, April 1955, pp. 225–8

Banham, R. 'Man, Machine and Motion' in *Architectural Review*, July 1955, pp. 51–3

Banham, R. 'Vehicles of Desire' in *Art*, 1 September 1955, p. 3

Banham, R. 'Industrial Design e Arte Populare' in *Civiltà delle Macchine*, November 1955, pp. 13–15

Banham, R. 'The New Brutalism' in *Architectural Review*, December 1955, pp. 354–61

Banham, R. 'Not Quite Architecture, Not Quite Painting or Sculpture Either' in *Architects Journal* 124, August 1956, pp. 217–21

Banham, R. 'This is Tomorrow' in *Architectural Review*, September 1956, pp. 186–8

Banham, R. 'This is Tomorrow: Synthesis of the Major Arts' in *Architectural Review*, 120, September 1956, pp. 186–8

Banham, R. 'Who Is Pop?' in *Motif*, winter 1962/3, pp. 3–13

Banham, R. 'The Atavism of the Short-Distance Mini-Cyclist' in *Living Arts*, No. 3, 1964, pp. 91–7

Banham, R. 'Detroit Tin Re-Visited' in *Design 1900–1960 – Studies in Design and Popular Culture*, Newcastle upon Tyne Polytechnic 1976, pp. 120–40

Bell, Q. 'Picasso and Picassini' in *The Listener*, 8 November 1951, p. 802

Berger, J. 'Present Painting' in *New Statesman and Nation*, 17 November 1951, p. 9

Brown, D. 'Refugee Artists in Britain' in *Art and Artists*, April 1984, pp. 6–10

Cordell, F. 'Gold Pan Alley: A Survey of the Popular Song Field' in *Ark* 19 March 1957, pp. 20–3

Crosby, T. 'This is Tomorrow' in *Architectural Design*, September 1956, pp. 302–4

Crosby, T. 'This is Tomorrow' in *Architectural Design*, October 1956, pp. 334–6

Davies, R. L. and Weeks, J. R. 'The Hertfordshire Achievement' in *Architectural Review*, June 1952, pp. 367–72 and 385–7

Fiedler, L. A. 'The Middle Against Both Ends' in *Encounter*, August 1955, pp. 16–23

Glaser, B. 'Three British Artists in New York' in *Studio International*, November 1965, pp. 178–83

Hamilton, R. 'Vision in Motion' in *Art*, London, 1, 5 January 1955, p. 3

Hamilton, R. 'Hommage à Chrysler Corps' in *Architectural Design*, March 1958, pp. 121–2

Hamilton, R. 'Persuading Image' in *Design*, February 1960, pp. 28–32

Hamilton, R. 'Popular Culture and Personal Responsibility' in *Design*, February 1961, p. 65

Hamilton, R. 'FOB +10' in *Design*, May 1961, pp. 40–51

Hamilton, R. '$he' in *Architectural Design*, October 1962 (reprinted in Russell and Gablik *Pop Art Redefined*, pp. 73–5)

Hamilton, R. 'Urbane Image' in *Living Arts*, 2 June 1963

Hamilton, R. 'Son of the Bride Stripped Bare' in *Art and Artists*, July 1966, pp. 22–8 (interview with Mario Amaya)

Hebdige, D. 'Towards a Cartography of Taste, 1935–1962' in *Block 4*, 1981, pp. 35–56

Hebdige, D. 'Object as Image: The Halian Scooter Cycle' in *Block 5*, 1981, pp. 44–6

Hebdige, D. 'In Poor Taste. Notes on Pop' in *Block 8*, 1983, pp. 54–68

Hodin, J. P. 'Summary of Events at ICA' in *Journal of Aesthetics and Art Criticism*, December 1953, pp. 278–82

Kauffmann, C. M. 'Taste and Opinion in England, 1920–1960' in *Art*, No. 30, pp. 13–17

Massey, A. 'Cold War Culture and the ICA' in *Art and Artists*, June 1984, pp. 15–17

Massey, A. 'The Independent Group as Design Theorists' in *From Spitfire to Microchip*, Design Council, 1985

Massey, A. 'The Independent Group and Modernism in Britain, 1951–1956' in *The Association of Art Historians Bulletin*, July 1984, pp. 23–4

Massey, A. 'The Independent Group: Towards a Redefinition' in *Burlington Magazine*, 129, April 1987, pp. 232–42

Massey, A. and Sparke, P. 'The Myth of the Independent Group' in *Block 10*, 1985, pp. 48–56

McHale, J. 'The Expendable Ikon 1' in *Architectural Design*, February 1959, pp. 82–3

McHale, J. 'The Expendable Ikon 2' in *Architectural Design*, March 1959, pp. 116–17

McHale, J. 'The Plastic Parthenon' in *Dotzero Magazine*, Spring 1967 (reprinted in Russell and Gablik, pp. 47–53)

McHale, J. 'The Fine Arts in the Mass Media' in *Cambridge Opinion*, No. 17, 1959 (reprinted in Russell and Gablik, pp. 43–7)

Melville, R. 'The Exhibitions of the ICA' in *The Studio*, April 1951, pp. 97–103

Nicholson, B. '1950, Aspects of British Art' in *New Statesman and Nation*, 23 December 1950, p. 8

Read, H. 'A Nest of Gentle Artists' in *Apollo*, September 1962, pp. 536–38

Reichardt, J. 'Pop Art and After' in *Art International*, February 1963, pp. 42–7

Reilly, P. 'Industry and the 1951 Festival' in *Design*, No. 2, February 1949, p. 1

Renzio, Toni del 'Shoes, Hair and Coffee' in *Ark*, 20, autumn 1957, pp. 27–30

Renzio, Toni del 'Style, Technique and Iconography' in *Art and Artists*, July 1976, pp. 35–8

Renzio, Toni del 'Pop' in *Art and Artists*, August 1976, pp. 15–19

Renzio, Toni del 'Pioneers and Trendies' in *Art and Artists*, March 1984, pp. 25–8

Robertson, B. 'Parallel of Life and Art' in *Art News and Review*, 19 September 1953, p. 6

Smithson, A. and P. 'But Today We Collect Ads' in *Ark*, No. 18, November 1957, pp. 48–50

Smithson, A. and P. 'Banham's Bumper Book on Brutalism' in *Architects Journal*, December 1966, pp. 1590–3

Sparke, P. 'Obituary: Peter Reyner Banham, 1922–1988' in *Journal of Design History 1*, 1988, p. 141

Sylvester, D. 'Art in a Coke Climate' in *Sunday Times Colour Supplement*, 26 January 1964, pp. 14–23

## Audio visual material

Arts Council, *Fathers of Pop*, video directed by Julian Cooper. Research by Penny Sparke, 1979

BBC, Reyner Banham, *Where Man Meets Machine*, talk transmitted on the Third Programme on 27 August 1955, BBC Written Archives

BBC, Reyner Banham, *Industrial Design and the Common User*, talk transmitted on the Third Programme on 26 April 1956, BBC Written Archives

BBC, *Art-Anti-Art*, series broadcast on the Third Programme starting 2 November 1959, produced by Leonie Cohn and introduced by Basil Taylor. Particularly programme number 6, broadcast 21 November 1959, 'Primitives of a Mechanised Art' by Reyner Banham, and number 15, 'Artists as Consumers: The Splendid Bargain', including Alloway, Paolozzi, Taylor and Hamilton in discussion. BBC Written Archives

BBC, *Pop Goes the Easel*, broadcast on 25 March 1962 on BBC Television, directed by Ken Russell. BBC Written Archives

BBC, Review of Lippard, L. *Pop Art* (1966) in *World of Books*, 14 February 1967. BBC Written Archives

Open University, Richard Hamilton, 'The Impact of American Pop Culture in the Fifties', Open University Tape A3515/16

## Unpublished sources

### Archives of the Arts Council of Great Britain

Confidential Minutes of the Meetings of the Executive Committee of the Arts Council of Great Britain from 18 July to 20 February 1952

Confidential Minutes of the Meetings of the Arts Council of Great Britain
from 15 August 1946 to 27 July 1955
Confidential Minutes of the Meetings of the Art Panel of the Arts Council
of Great Britain from 16 August 1946 to 20 April 1956
Council Papers Numbers 226, 247 and 298
Correspondence and memoranda

### A. H. Barr Papers, Museum of Modern Art, New York

Correspondence relating to the Unknown Political Prisoner Competition

### Archives of the British Council Art Department

Correspondence relating to Herbert Read, Roland Penrose and official
policy

### Archives of the Design Council

Correspondence, memoranda and reports concerning the *Britain Can Make
It* and *Festival of Britain* exhibitions

### Archives of the Institute of Contemporary Arts

Minutes of the Meetings of the ICA Organising Committee from 30
January 1946 to 17 June 1948
Minutes of the Meetings of the Growth and Form Exhibition Sub-
Committee from 31 January 1950 to 15 September 1950
Minutes of the Meetings of the Lecture Sub-Committee from January
1952 to 11 May 1954
Minutes of the Meetings of the ICA Managing Committee from 21
September 1948 to 20 December 1956
Minutes of the Meetings of the Exhibition Sub-Committee from 15
February 1950 to 17 June 1956
Transcriptions of interviews by Dorothy Morland of: Joan Edwards (19
June 1978), Richard Hamilton (undated), Anthony Hill (undated),
Richard Lannoy (undated), Roland Penrose (October 1976)
The reminiscences of: George Hoellering (26 January 1977), Dorothy
Morland (undated), Julie Lawson (27 January 1977), Brenda Pool
(undated)

## Transcriptions of discussions, lectures and speeches

*Painting, Sculpture and the Architect*, lecture by Siegfried Giedion dated 18
August 1948
*The Industrial Designer and Public Taste*, discussion chaired by Misha
Black dated 7 February 1950
*The Strange Case of Abstract Art*, discussion chaired by Herbert Read
dated 14 March 1950

*The Function and Aims of an Institute of Contemporary Arts*, discussion chaired by J. M. Richards dated 18 April 1950

*Public View No. 1 Works by Orneore Metelli from the Hanover Gallery and by Victor Pasmore from the Redfern Gallery*, discussion chaired by A. D. B. Sylvester dated 9 January 1951

*The Shape of Science in the Arts*, lecture by Dr J. Bronowski dated 2 August 1951

*Painting and the Future of Painting*, lecture by Man Ray dated 27 October 1954

Opening Remarks by Le Corbusier at the *Growth and Form* exhibition (undated)

### Reports and correspondence, Archive of Newcastle upon Tyne University

Correspondence and memoranda relating to *Man, Machine and Motion Exhibition*

### Archives of Roland Penrose

Letters between Roland Penrose and Herbert Read relating to the ICA

### Archives of the Royal College of Art (with special thanks to Penny Sparke)

Material collected for the *Fathers of Pop* (1979) but largely unused

Transcription of interview by Julian Cooper of John McHale (undated)

Transcriptions of interviews by Reyner Banham of: Lawrence Alloway (25 May 1977), Frank Cordell, Richard Hamilton, Nigel Henderson, Dorothy Morland, Richard Smith, Peter & Alison Smithson, William Turnbull (all undated)

Transcriptions of discussions between: Mary and Reyner Banham, John McHale, Magda Cordell dated 30 May 1977; Toni del Renzio, Reyner Banham and Richard Hamilton (undated)

### Tate Gallery Archives

Material relating to *This is Tomorrow*, Richard Hamilton and Nigel Henderson

### Victoria and Albert Museum, the Art and Design Archives

Collection of Paolozzi's Krazy Kat Archive material

# Index